THE SURFACE EFFECT

Even before we think, we use fantasy. Is fantasy the 'mother of all media'? Does fantasy save me from myself? Are there fictions that are real?

In *The Surface Effect* André Nusselder examines the space of fantasy between individual 'inner life' and social 'outer life'. Where we assume that fantasy only operates where we float off in imaginary realms, this book shows that we are in it from the beginning.

Based on the work of Jacques Lacan, Nusselder elaborates Lacan's theory, showing how the effects of unconscious processes converge in fantasy as our principal medium for intersubjectivity, self-identity, and remembering. The human mind is seen as a composite function of language, body and social world, and fantasy is the fundamental process to study this effect.

The book is divided into three sections:

- the philosophical context
- Lacan's theory of fantasy
- Lacan and philosophy.

The Surface Effect analyses fantasy as a medium, both creative and protective operating between anxiety and excess. It focuses on the role of fantasy in psychoanalysis, and follows its path towards reflections on mediation and new media. This book will appeal to psychoanalysts, philosophers, cognitive scientists and those studying new media, film, culture and literature.

André Nusselder is a Dutch philosopher.

THE SURFACE EFFECT

The screen of fantasy in psychoanalysis

André Nusselder

Routledge
Taylor & Francis Group
LONDON AND NEW YORK

First published 2013 by Routledge
27 Church Road, Hove, East Sussex BN3 2FA
711 Third Avenue, New York NY 10017

Routledge is an imprint of the Taylor & Francis Group, an informa business

British Library Cataloguing in Publication Data
A catalogue record for this book is available from the British Library

Library of Congress Cataloging in Publication Data
Nusselder, André.
The surface effect: the screen of fantasy in psychoanalysis / André Nusselder.
p. cm.
Includes bibliographical references.
ISBN 978-0-415-69280-9 (hardback)—
ISBN 978-0-415-69281-6 (paperback) 1. Fantasy.
2. Subconsciousness. 3. Psychoanalysis. I. Title.
BF175.5.F36N87 2012
154.3—dc23

2012006863

ISBN: 978-0-415-69280-9 (hbk)
ISBN: 978-0-415-69281-6 (pbk)
ISBN: 978-0-203-10148-3 (ebk)

Typeset in Garamond
by RefineCatch Limited, Bungay, Suffolk

IN MEMORY OF MY FATHER: HENK NUSSELDER

What, then, happens in the soul when it takes more delight at finding or having restored to it the things it loves than if it had always possessed them?

(Augustine, *Confessions*, Book Eight, ch. 3, 7)

CONTENTS

INTRODUCTION

Fantasy as the place where we live[1]

We inhabit a world of surfaces. When in love, we present ourselves to our beloved as attractively as we can. At a job interview, we try to impress the interviewer by saying some things that we can hardly live up to – so that afterwards we have to run with this image and may achieve things we did not even know were possible. Also, in a struggle, we make ourselves bigger than we are to intimidate the other person. This role of the surface even appears to increase in a life full of media technologies. Increasingly, we meet our friends on Facebook, and our web profile may be very 'superficial' but nevertheless has very real effects. These examples show that a human being is divided 'between its being and its semblance' (Lacan 1998b: 107). Nevertheless, it 'is through this separated form of himself that the being comes into play in his effects' (ibid.). Apparently, semblance is involved where our being is at stake, and human consciousness is largely a matter of effects.

> I hope you'll consider consciousness to occur each time – and it occurs in the most unexpected and disparate places – there's a surface such that it can reproduce what is called *an image*.
>
> (Lacan 1988b: 49)

> It is useful, then, to think of a third area of human living, one neither inside the individual nor outside in the world of shared reality.
>
> (Winnicott 1971: 110)

The intermediary space between individual 'inner life' and social 'outer life' (their interface or surface) is an important space for human existence and development. Here, I seek to describe this space by presenting fantasy in the work of Lacan as the primary medium for the subject of desire. Although at first sight fantasy seems to be nothing but an imaginary duplication, its images are always related to others, so that the 'double' is included from the start in the signifying order of intersubjective relations. Thus, the crucial question about the image (in mimicry) is: What effects does it have on the other, what does it mean to her?

Fantasy consists of the order of images *and* that of meaning. This conception of fantasy is, for Lacan – who thinks linguistic elements are the primary building blocks of our being, crucial for understanding the unconscious dimension of fantasy. Because signifiers work in it, fantasy is more than a mirror-image or reflection of the real: it is also a (symbolic) construction of it. Such fantasmatic constructions of the real are at the heart of psychical reality. In the unconscious mind, fantasy therefore is the 'script' of the role that we play.

Another core function of fantasy is to provide pleasure. Maybe this is even its 'real core', as this function intimately connects it to the body and its physical environment. What is real and how fantasy relates to it is a difficult question. From a psychoanalytic point of view, the real is thought of as traumatic, as an unbearable affection that calls for defensive mechanisms. These defensive mechanisms are also at work in fantasy. So the fantasy-images that provide pleasure are at the same time a defence against what Lacan calls a traumatic realm of enjoyment (*jouissance*).

The 'image' in fantasy thus covers several dimensions, including those of pleasure and enjoyment, of signification, and of protection. This book tries to systematically unravel these aspects of fantasy in the work of Lacan. In doing so, it brings to the fore that fantasy is not just an imaginary duplication of human reality but actually its condition. Here we meet the 'productive' aspect of fantasy as hinted upon in the work of Freud and in some philosophical traditions.

Freud's remark that there is a fundamental difference between erotic life in the ancient world and in our modern one points to this productive role of fantasy. Where the ancients emphasized the drive, and so could honour even inferior objects, we despise libidinal activity and place all value in the object itself (Freud 1905: 149fn.). We, modern people, believe that what arouses our desire are the inherent qualities in the beloved person – thus passing over the pulsional activities that underlie the elevated and idealized status of the beloved one. What we ignore is the role of fantasy as a principal medium itself, as a medium that grounds in pulsional activity and transfers the 'value' that it seeks as belonging to the object itself. This is probably one of the most important lessons that Freudian psychoanalysis can teach us and makes comprehensible why fantasy is the fundamental object of psychoanalysis (Laplanche and Pontalis 1986: 14).[2]

Fantasy is an ineffaceable medium in perception, recollection, and even in human understanding. It is the medium between object and subject. Fantasy is, to put it in the words of Winnicott, a 'third area', at the surface of self and other, interfacing individual and world. Much constructive work takes place in this intermediary space, where the inner life of the individual and the outer world meet. The classical distinction of reality and illusion is therefore too narrow for psychoanalytical interpretation.

As this constructive work is to a large extent unconscious, the subject of consciousness is fundamentally split, and has an uncanny twin brother.

Sometimes it can see what its rival is up to, sometimes this is not so clear, and maybe they even share a common ground. So I may well be aware of the fact that I write a fantasy-scenario and play the role of its main character: the daydream is the most obvious example of the relation between consciousness and the unconscious. In such a (conscious) fantasy, it is still recognizable that the subject turns itself into a fantasy-object that it is not. However, there may also be mechanisms so subtle and hidden that we do not know that we turn ourselves into an object. What exactly do we know of our most intimate self-representations, of why we strive for a particular thing, why we said something that we later regret, performed a certain stupid act, or enjoyed playing a specific role? These (fantasmatic) appearances not only dodge consciousness, they are also what we are most intimately connected to. For Lacan, the unconscious is not merely an 'incommunicable inwardness'. He focuses rather on the exterior form of our intimacy, which leads him to the neologism extimacy (*extimité*): the unconscious is outside. 'The extimate, like the intimate, is that which is the most hidden . . . in both cases this is also for the subject what is closest to him' (Guéguen 2006: 270).

What I try to do in this book is to think fantasy in its unconscious dimension, and beyond the process of neurotic repression. For the most intricate and interesting functioning of fantasy can be found where it already influences our identity, perception, and remembering without us being aware of it, and without it being merely a neurotic compensation. The analysis of fantasy thus exceeds the model of *Versagung* ('frustration'). Fantasy is more than the result of an unsatisfactory reality. Such a frustration characterizes the neurotic: reality is so unsatisfying that the neurotic tries to compensate for it in his imaginary inside world of fantasies. And the psychotic goes a long way towards replacing the outside world by his fantasmatic fabrications. However, this work seeks to think fantasy beyond these pathological formations, as the *condition of desire* – a difficult task, as it forces us to go to a deep psychological level where fantasy and reality are not merely opposites. An example may be illuminating here.

Let us suggest that I am playing in a virtual world on the Internet and stroll around with my avatar (virtual personae) in a fantasmatic scenario that makes me laugh. The question then is, who is actually laughing: my 'virtual' or my 'real' self? And the same question may be posed when I, in Real Life, later tell my funny story in Second Life to someone and again I must laugh. Who actually is laughing then: the self here and now, or the self of the fantasmatic scenario? The answer, which takes us to the position that I elaborate in this book, is probably 'both'. The two selves are intricately connected, maybe even the same!

The fundamental intuition that I try to follow in this book is that the core of our psychic life is taking place at the surface, where each of us is a subject (of 'imagination') turned into an object (of fantasy) – that is, fundamentally mediated by fantasy. Fantasy, in its function of being the condition of desire, is the place where we are both the *writer* of a fantasy-scenario and its *protagonist*. For a divided subject playing two roles, fantasy is closely related to the perverse position (that centres on such duplicities). At a 'deep psychological' level, fantasy is a medium that makes the subject of desire stick so close to the object that it turns itself into, that it is hard to see them as separated (this is the fundamental fantasy). Here fantasy reaches a level that goes beyond repression and pathology. 'No access to the object without the mediation of fantasy: this is what seals the modern unconscious cult of the object, via the fantasmatic medium' (Assoun 2007: 96; my translation). Because of this transcendental aspect of fantasy, I also turn to the philosophical tradition.

One of the most important themes in philosophy is the mediation of the subject and the object. For a long period in Western history, this mediation was ignored and scientists believed in immediate access to presence. In the tradition of Platonism, whose offspring we can recognize nowadays in the revival of all sorts of beliefs in immediacy (religious, technological), there is a belief in a direct 'contact point' between representation and its object, without the 'disturbance' of subjectivity. For the philosopher Jacques Derrida, this desire for unmediated 'presence' makes Western philosophy largely a 'philosophy of presence': a philosophy guaranteed by some sort of Logos (Reason or God) that ignores processes of mediation (Derrida 1976).

The tradition of Platonism changed its clothes with the rise of modern science and technology in early modern Western history. The philosophy of René Descartes is its most profound articulation. It considers true knowledge not to be present in some sort of higher ontological domain (as in Platonism), but still attainable through the accuracy of human thinking and representation. Modern science and philosophy calculates the world as it appears in the mirror of consciousness. For that reason, it is a 'philosophy of consciousness'. The philosopher Martin Heidegger names the modern world the 'Age of the World Picture' where knowledge is only accepted as true when it is true for the knowing subject.

The critical philosophy of Immanuel Kant elaborated the crucial question whether modern consciousness does not merely represent the things as they appear to us and not as they are in themselves: it caused a 'crack' in the homogeneity of the World Picture. Heidegger, who followed this Kantian inspiration, subsequently labels the modern subject a 'philosophical dreamer', trapped in his own fantasies, which it takes for reality. What is needed, therefore, is the analysis of the hidden, underlying layers of consciousness itself (unconscious subjectivity). Psychoanalysis is a major tradition in this analysis.

What distinguishes psychoanalytical research from philosophical analyses of representation is its study of representation against the (catastrophic) background of anxiety: the crucial affection of psychoanalytical practice. From a psychoanalytical perspective, the human condition is a tragic one. According to Lacan, psychoanalysis would lose its relevance even when one forgets this tragedy – which might account for the diminished position of psychoanalysis in current (technological) society that thinks of finding a solution to every problem. In the tragic situation that psychoanalysis studies, fantasy is an inevitable distanciation from the real. We need culture, sublimation, surfaces, practices, and places where we organize surplus forms of enjoyment that 'cultivate' an excessive *jouissance*, a tension that exceeds the pleasure principle. We should not forget that (erotic) desire is never far removed from the death drive.

Such surfaces are the framework for the subject's libidinal relation to the outside world. Just as in a competitive battle, the blown-up image that a person presents to its rival is the framework for this intersubjective relation. The place where we live is in the effects of the fantasmatic framework.

Part I

THE PHILOSOPHICAL CONTEXT

1

LOVE AND LANGUAGE

1.1 Platonism

Eros and nostalgia: real beauty

In nostalgia, our thoughts return to a certain environment or to a long-gone period of our life. In those recurring thoughts we feel that we return home. Or, at least we feel *as if* we are returning home to the environment in which our desires seemed fulfilled. In nostalgia, we experience an imaginary world parallel to our desires; in our imagination there appears to be such a parallel world. But was this world ever real or is it rather an echo of our own desire for moments of fulfilment? Is our memory of it true or imbued by illusion? In short, was there ever such a 'home'?

Although the 'lost world' may never have been real, nostalgia shows that the *psychic experience* of such a 'home' is a fact. Although the situation in the past to which we refer is long gone, my recollection pretends to represent what the original situation signifies. There is the suggestion of a resemblance, imitation, or even unity between the element of representation and the 'original', a suggestion of their immediate relationship. A similar 'ideal reminiscence' is at work in Plato's theory of knowledge, which is at the roots of Western thought.

In *The Symposium*, Plato gives a glorious account of love. The guests he introduces at Agathon's dinner discuss the god Eros and delineate what is now known as the Platonic concept of love. Through Aristophanes, Plato formulates a myth about the original human body (with four legs and arms) that Zeus, as a punishment for man's attempts to attack the gods, cuts in half in order to weaken mankind. Eros is the desire of the split human being for its Other half: the desire to become One again. Platonic Eros is the inner tension that makes us aspire and desire for the beautiful, for it is beauty, in all its manifestations, that love aims at. Happiness results from a perfectly realized love that makes us return to our original state and thus 'heals' us.

For Plato, a (re)finding of beauty in a particular thing is seen as a reference to beauty in general: physical beauty refers to spiritual beauty, and the beauty of social institutions refers to the beauty of knowledge and science. Platonic Eros is a desire that refers to Beauty itself and finds its final aim in its contemplation. This Beauty, of which all other things partake, really exists in a higher ontological domain, so that the desire for it is not principally unrealizable. Man can realize his basic 'nostalgic' desire, which continuously causes him to search further and further, in the contemplation of the archetype of all that is beautiful: the Form of Beauty.

The reification of meaning

The metaphysical assumption of an original plenitude that guarantees the meaning of representations is the foundation of true knowledge. One often refers to this Platonic basis of Occidental thought as 'metaphysics of presence'. Jacques Derrida, who continues the Heideggerian critique on this metaphysics, allies the original presence with Logos, God, and teleology (Derrida 1976).[1] According to Plato, the human mind knew of this original plenitude before it was incarnated into a body, as a result of which it was 'forgotten'. Recollection would retrieve this essential knowledge, and the theory of reminiscence or recollection (*anamnesis*) is hence pivotal for the claim on true knowledge.[2]

In the philosophy of language, this Platonist philosophy became the foundation of the 'classical' theory of meaning. This theory holds that words directly express meaning. Language supposedly names concepts (Ideas) that exist independently of being named: a statement is only true when it corresponds to an extra-linguistic reality. Plato hence upholds a theory of truth as correspondence. In the influential semantics of St. Augustine, Platonism came to imply that a person could retrieve the meaning of a word by finding out what it refers to. In his description of himself as a child, St. Augustine brings forward that he could retrieve the meaning of a word by observing the gestures and facial expressions that the adults used to indicate an object. As the facial expressions of the adults would exactly show what they mean, without deformation or distortion in the process of representation, the representations show us the meaning of the object they refer to. In the classical theory of meaning (Plato, St. Augustine, Frege), meaning is a thing that exists objectively, independently of the subject and of the manner ('media') in which it is articulated. Due to this *reification* of meaning, a philosopher of the classical school can think meaning as that which characterizes the essence of the reference.

The desire for immediacy

Ever since its debut in Western history, philosophical speculation was led by notions of direct vision, intuition, and sight. In contrast to the (indirect) knowledge that we collect in all sorts of discourses, this 'sight' would provide direct knowledge. The Platonic origin of this notion of 'view' or 'sight' ('theoria') asserts that the object of knowledge resembles the object of view in its true form. In Plato's thinking, we find an immediate relationship between representation and its content, a contact point that is thought in terms of light – not in a mere physical sense, but in a metaphysical one. Plato's famous allegory of the cave expresses this (metaphysical) desire for illumination. The persons in the cave aspire to see the light of the sun and to free themselves from their physical position in the cave in which they see nothing but the shadows of things on the wall.

The decisive point of Platonism is its transformation of transcendence (what surpasses our knowledge and vision, and hence is what our desire is directed at) into an object that can be 'seen' by the 'eye of the soul'. Similarly, Plato turns light, that which gives all else visibility, into an object – a conception that the ancients had never used before (Hillis 1999: 138). Light, therefore, is the crucial contact point between subject and object. Not surprisingly, the Platonic metaphysics that grounded the Western world is a 'metaphysics of light' (Blumenberg 1993: 33).

We can find this metaphysics of immediacy in the supposed 'realism' of photography. We tend to believe the photographic image as a representation of reality not distorted by subjectivity. Many theorists of photography, from Talbot to Bazin to Barthes, consider light to be the contact point that establishes an immediate relationship between photograph and object. We believe in the immediate relationship between the object and the picture, especially the photographic picture, but also those of painting, film, television, and digital graphics.[3] 'The common feature of all of these forms is the belief in some necessary contact point between the medium and what it represents' (Bolter and Grusin 2000: 30). The aspiration for immediacy is, at least since the Renaissance, a defining feature of Western visual representation.

Platonism is also at work in our current media society. The world of digital information and communication (cyberspace) is likely to be considered as independent from all the computers and networks that provide access to it. Thus thought of as an independent realm of data, cyberspace resembles the Platonic realm of ideas of which the objects in our reality are nothing but a pale copy. As we primarily explore this parallel world of information mentally, it also reproduces the Platonic dualism of body and mind.

The Platonic tradition of 'neglecting' the subjectivity of the body, of the imagination, of language, and of our tools, was carried on in the modern 'philosophy of consciousness'. However, the modern tradition puts forward the rational subject as a firm ground for true knowledge.

Reflection as a philosophical dream?

The Platonism of 'pure sight' is a kind of *passive* representation (contemplation). It certainly is not the *active* representation or putting forward, and one might even use the terms 'production' or 'performance', that according to Heidegger is so characteristic of modern thought (Heidegger 1997). Western modernity brings forth the thinking subject. As a consequence of the Cartesian *cogito ergo sum* ('I think, therefore I am') this thinking subject is characterized by a rupture between itself and the material world. For Descartes, there are two kinds of substance: *res cogitans*, thinking substance (mind or soul), and *res extensa*, extended substance (body). It is the thinking subject that grounds truth: something is only true when it is true for this rational subject. Being is identified with 'being represented'.[4]

According to Heidegger, the modern age is therefore 'the age of the world picture'. The essence of the modern age is the becoming image of the world. The modern science that Descartes helped to set up posits the human subject at a centrally located point: as the guarantee of the certainty of knowledge. Heidegger connects this decisive transition in the Western world to a crucial difference in the status of fantasy. In (pre-Socratic) Greek thought, fantasy ('phantasia') still concerns the 'coming into appearance' of Being: it reveals something of the secrecy of Being. Modern man, however, who has turned the world into an image, merely *fantasizes*. For Heidegger, this modern subject of representation is a philosophical dreamer. It thinks the world is as imagined by him:

> Man as representing subject, however 'fantasizes', i.e., he moves in *imaginatio*, in that his representing imagines, pictures forth, whatever is, as the objective, into the world as picture.
>
> (Heidegger 1997: 147)[5]

It is from hereon that we may come to understand the impact of the Freudian discovery on the philosophy of consciousness.

1.2 Freudism[6]

Representation and the unconscious

In his book, *Imagination and the Meaningful Brain*, Harvard psychiatrist Arnold Modell states: 'The mind/brain does not represent or mirror reality; it *constructs* a virtual reality of its own' (Modell 2006: 13). Freud's 'discovery' of the unconscious was a major factor in the questioning of the mind as an accurate 'representation machine' of reality. Freud's work demonstrated that recollections are not unaffected by our libidinal life.

Memory is not like a chest of drawers where information is stored in the drawers that can be opened to see what is inside (Modell 1996). Memory represents the inscriptions of the past in accordance with our current beliefs, goals, and desires (Lamm 1993; Schacter and Scarry 1998). These insights on the close connection of memory and the unconscious are extended both in current psychoanalytic theories (Morris 1993; Laplanche and Pontalis 1998) and in those of cognitive science. Memory is transcriptive and an active process of construction (Edelman 1992; Freeman 1995).

Freud's thinking of unconscious representation started with considering 'inscriptions' being made on 'another scene'. According to Freud, events not only get an inscription in the human mind by means of 'word representations' ('Wortvorstellungen') on the (pre)conscious level; there are also 'thing representations' ('Sachvorstellungen') on the unconscious level. These unconscious representations are memory traces of objects or events that are relevant to the drives ('satisfaction'). The rules that govern unconscious representations (primary process) do not follow the same logic as those of (pre)conscious representations (secondary process). In the (unconscious) primary processes, energy floats freely and is not hindered by the signs or pieces of evidence from outer reality. Therefore, the affection of a representation can easily be displaced to another representation (the mechanism of *displacement*, or 'Verschiebung'), and one representation can collect the affections of several representations (*condensation*, or *Verdichtung*). In the unconscious, energy is not inhibited due to a binding to certain (acceptable) representations. The primary process does not know of time and logical contradictions: it simply strives for an 'identity of perception' to satisfy its primitive wishes (in a hallucinatory way); it does not aim at an 'identity of thought' as in the secondary process. The unconscious reservoir of libido, the Id, does not know of moral evaluations, and knows no good and evil. These inscriptions in the unconscious may explain, for example, why we seek to go back to a certain event or person although we consciously know it would be better to stay away from it (repetition).

Unconscious inscriptions direct our recollections. The recollections Freud was confronted with in his clinical practice often concerned issues of (sexual) excitement. Representations of excitement were *repressed* into the unconscious because they were either unacceptable to the moral self (the Superego), or the intrusion of excitement was so great (i.e. traumatic) that the psychical apparatus could not (sufficiently) bind it to representations, so that the energy of the event remained a haunting threat in the unconscious. This 'excess' of energy that is not sufficiently bound to 'word representations' floats freely in the unconscious, where it keeps on working and may attach itself capriciously – according to the mechanisms of displacement and condensation – to certain word representations. Those (pre)conscious word representations (a certain memory-image, idea or word) then have a large libidinal investment in the unconscious, which may explain why someone's psychical life gravitates around certain recurring ideas.[7] Although Freud in his early work thought that it was possible to recollect, and thereby discharge the traumatic events responsible for such 'unbalanced representations' (Josef Breuer's 'cathartic method'), he soon came to realize that psychical reality is not necessarily a representation of actual events. Freud abandoned his early theory of seduction that assigned a crucial role in the production of neuroses to memories of actual seduction attempts. Even without (transgressive) acts, 'sexuality' was a problem (cf. Van Haute and Geyskens 2004).

Psychical reality as a knot of real and fictional elements

In the earlier formulations of his theory, Freud considers fantasies as having been made unconscious by means of 'forgetting' or defence. He considers the symptoms of his first (hysterical) patients as the result of fantasies that were conscious first and later made unconscious. So if the therapy might bring to light the real events in infantile life that gave rise to these first conscious fantasies, the unconscious fantasy might loosen its grip on the patient. At the outset of his development of psychoanalysis, Freud devotes his labour (for which he even uses hypnosis) to the process of remembering. At that time, he still understands the real cause of mental states in a scientific-positivistic manner, as a fact in reality. But this was soon to change.

Because of his shocking discovery that infantile scenes are not always true, Freud has to revise his idea that the analysis of symptoms reveals the infantile scenes that had actually taken place and that fixate the libido and determine the symptoms. He discovers that symptoms can also be representations of fantasies. Of those fantasies Freud says:

> They too possess a reality of a sort. It remains a fact that the patient has created these phantasies for himself, and this fact is of scarcely less importance for his neurosis than if he had really experienced what the phantasies contain. The phantasies possess *psychical* as contrasted with *material* reality, and we gradually learn to understand that *in the world of the neurosis it is psychical reality which is the decisive kind.*
>
> (Freud 1917: 368)

Thus Freud repeats in 1917, in the twenty-third of his *Introductory Lectures on Psychoanalysis*, the decisive discovery that he first formulates in his famous letter to Wilhelm Fliess of 21 September 1897. In that letter he declares that he no longer believes his neurotic patients. Several arguments led to this conclusion: First, the impossibility of bringing the analysis to a real conclusion. Second, the improbability that every scene of seduction, that so many of his patients came up with, really occurred: the perversity of 'uncles' towards children could not be that widespread. Freud distances himself from his previous theory of seduction. Third, the discovery that there are no indications of reality in the unconscious, so that one cannot distinguish between truth and fiction that is cathected with affection (Freud 1892–1899: 260). Fourth, the consideration that even in the deepest psychosis the unconscious memory does not overcome the resistance of the conscious, so that there is no reason to expect that in treatment the conscious will completely tame the unconscious.

Between 1895 and 1899, the years that completed the discovery of psychoanalysis, Freud abandons his theory of seduction. He no longer believes that a trauma that really took place, the seduction by the father or the 'uncle', was the cause of hysteria. Instead, he discovers the (auto-)erotic impulses of childhood (cf. Verhaeghe 1999: 28). The scene of seduction is not (necessarily) a truthful representation of an event, but often moulded by a fantasy that functions as a cover up of the spontaneous manifestations of sexual activity! The seduction is a tangle, a knot, of real and fictional elements (where 'real' increasingly refers to the 'impulses' instead of to a 'historical reality').[8] In his *History of the Psychoanalytic Movement,* Freud formulates his decisive discovery as follows:

> If hysterical subjects trace back their symptoms to traumas that are fictitious, then the new fact which emerges is precisely that they create such scenes in *fantasy*, and this psychical reality requires to be taken into account alongside practical reality. This reflection was soon followed by the discovery that these fantasies were intended to cover up the autoerotic activity of the first years of childhood, to embellish it and raise it to a higher plane. And now, from behind the fantasies, the whole range of a child's sexual life came to light.
>
> (Freud, in Laplanche and Pontalis 1986: 8)

Freud discovers a connection between sexuality, trauma and defence, and his intention was to show that it is in the very nature of sexuality to have a traumatic effect (Laplanche and Pontalis 1986: 9).

In the years that followed his discovery of the importance of fantasies in psychic life, Freud is taken up by the problem of memory and its distortions (through fantasies). In 1899, he publishes his findings on the defensive functions of some memories. In his analysis of his own memories of childhood in 'Screen Memories' (1899), he advances the idea that some memories intermingle elements of memory – although in general detached from their contexts – and elements of fantasy. Although they defend the subject against the memory of a traumatic experience, they nevertheless express the infantile element that is so emotionally charged, by concentrating it on a fixed and objectified form (cf. Perron-Borelli 2001: 22). Freud finds memories to function as a cover-up of early sexual activities or fantasies. And where he initially thought of this sexuality as the seduction by an adult, he later finds it was the auto-erotic impulses of the child itself. So screen-memories function as a defence against a sexuality that is unacceptable for the ego: 'there was no childhood memory, but only a phantasy put back into childhood' (Freud 1899: 315). Childhood memories involve complicated processes of remodelling. Freud compares this to the process by which a nation constructs legends about its early history.

Language and the montage of the drive

We speak of a wish (Freud) or of desire (Lacan) when the object that provides satisfaction (to the drives) is articulated in 'language'. Freud's interpretation of dreams as the fulfilment of a wish is the most obvious example of this: unconscious 'dream thoughts' are expressed through the special 'language' of dreams. With language, and this is where Lacan surpasses Freud (into the field of philosophy), a *subject* of desire arises (cf. Lacan 1998b: 178–179). The term 'subject' does not appear in Freud's work, and is more widely used in disciplines like philosophy, linguistics, and law. That Lacan uses this term indicates his shift towards those disciplines in the elaboration of the unconscious.

The source of the drive is somatical, grounded in the physiological processes of the body. Nevertheless, psychoanalysis focuses on its mental representations. The drive is at the border of the somatical and the mental (Freud 1915a). The object of the drive is therefore not an immediate 'biological' given but also a cultural construct, a pleasure assembled or even staged under the demands of outside reality. Freud stresses that the aspiration for pleasurable discharge (the pleasure principle) is, most of the time, controlled by processes of thinking (the reality principle). These (secondary) processes of thought are nevertheless only a temporary and necessary detour for achieving the pleasurable discharge of tensions. The reality principle is in the service of the pleasure principle – its detour gives the pleasure-providing object a 'cultural' appearance (sublimation).[9]

Also for Lacan, the drives do not know of some sort of mythical or natural satisfaction. First, because the different partial drives (i.e. originating in different erogenous zones of the body) cannot be unified once and for all under the primacy of the genital zone (a 'genital drive'). Genital sexuality, as the supposed 'maturation' of sexual development, is therefore always a precarious affair (cf. Evans 1996: 47). Second, as the object of a drive is a thoroughly cultural and symbolic construct, thinking the satisfaction of the drive leads us to the category of the impossible (Lacan 1998b: 166). What the different partial drives aim at is to perpetually circle around the unattainable object of satisfaction (Lacan 1998b: 168). Also, here Lacan takes into the field of linguistics Freud's definition of the drive as a montage, consisting of four elements: the pressure, the end, the object, and the source. Emphasizing the linguistic elements in the 'montage' of the drive moves Lacan's theories away from what he considers the 'biological aberrations' in psychoanalysis. It does not leave the body behind, but considers it as a 'libidinal body' where body and language intermingle into a concept of libido that is a matter of a somatic force and its linguistic construction. Energy is not the basic concept for understanding human being, but linguistic information. 'Don't you know that the energetic is nothing else . . . than the appliance of a network of signifiers onto the world?' (Lacan 1991: 54; my translation).

The unconscious subject of desire consists of imaginary and symbolic identifications (the theme of Chapter 3). By means of these identifications there is a (virtual) unitary form to its desire. The subject turns itself into an object: the self as an object in the mirror illustrates this. Or it turns the other into an object: we assume that the other is as she is *for us*. So the subject introduces a unity that does not exist 'in the real' (and fantasy is the primary medium between the real and the virtual). Nostalgia illustrates this: the best way to annihilate this fabrication at the surface of reality and desire is to invent a time-machine and travel back in time to find out that there is no 'real reality' corresponding to the ideal representation we made of it – and that we made the representation up of bits and pieces.

For Lacan, those 'bits and pieces' consist primarily of linguistic elements called 'signifiers': material, 'acoustic images' we use to signify things. By means of fantasy, we synthesize those 'bits and pieces' into a (meaningful) whole. The notion of the signifier indicates where we must seek for the unconscious aspect of fantasy: not in some sort of 'dark inwardness' but in the linguistic elements of (unconscious) thought. The difficult claim of Lacanian psychoanalysis is to see how signifiers govern the unconscious, how they mould – outside of our conscious awareness – the object that we desire.

As the unconscious is for Lacan such a matter of linguistic construction, I will first discuss the science of signs – semiotics – so that it becomes clear in what kind of radical break with classical theories of meaning and representation Lacan's form of Freudism must be situated.

1.3 Saussurism[10]

Presence and the sign

Since the beginning of Western thought, perhaps even since the origin of mankind itself, man has realized that the exchange of meaningful messages is a mediated process consisting of the transmission, reception, and recognition of signs. The sign, as it is generally understood, refers to something different from itself. It presents the object in its absence. The best known system of signs, spoken language, is therefore a medium that relates us to 'objects' (things, persons, worlds, ideas, intentions, etc.) that are not immediately present. Presence, or what we are inclined to call reality, is mediated by the sign, at the surface (for that reason, Plato considered signs as deceptive, superficial 'things').

The study of signs leads to the pressing question whether there is a reality outside the signs at all. The work of the French sociologist Jean Baudrillard (1929–2007) shows how crucial this question is to our so-called post-modern era, wherein this mediating function of the sign is acknowledged: there is a 'breach of contact' between language and reality (Lyotard 1986; Steiner 1989). Jean Francois Lyotard's 'theory of delegitimization' shows that contemporary thought can no longer rely upon the idea of a human rationality (in science or philosophy) that legitimizes tales of 'true' representation. Baudrillard speaks of a 'murder of reality', which is not just the result of media-technologies hiding the real behind a screen of images, but especially of 'real time' communication destroying the illusion (the 'other scene') that is vital to reality.

Baudrillard's work is an analysis of the supposed disappearance of this 'other scene', of the unconscious. When there is no Other, everything becomes the Same. This is how he starts his book *The Perfect Crime*:

> This is the story of a crime – of the murder of reality. And the extermination of an illusion – the vital illusion, the radical illusion of the world. The real does not disappear into illusion; it is illusion that disappears into reality.
>
> (Baudrillard 1996)

There are three different philosophical positions concerning the relation of sign and reality. *Idealism* holds that signs construct our perception of reality, which subsequently is purely subjective. The subject constitutes reality like a projector in a cinema projects the objects on the screen. The subject not only *projects* reality, but it also *perceives* what it projects. Then there is nothing but signs, or to put it in the notorious words of Jacques Derrida: 'there is nothing outside the text' (Derrida 1976: 158). There is no 'transcendent signified' (Derrida 1976: 20; 1978: 278–280). In linguistic relativism (that some call a post-modern form of idealism), there is no independent ('real') reality outside sign systems. An odd agent of a 'post-modern idealism' is Lewis Carroll's character Humpty Dumpty, who thinks that he himself can determine the meaning of his words, without being limited by any sort of reference.

The extreme opposite of this idealistic position is *realism*. As the more common-sense approach, it holds that a single objective reality is present outside us. It parallels so-called 'language-word isomorphism', which considers correspondence between sign and referent to be a one-to-one relationship. In realism, ideas and concepts are mental reproductions of real things in the world. The subject must conform to the object to attain true knowledge. Photography illustrates realism's aspiration of recording the object as it really is.

Constructivism is the intermediate position between idealism and realism. It considers language – and every system of signs – to play an important role in our sense of reality. Constructivism does not eliminate the reality of the outside world, as idealism, or simply pose it as something barely affected by the sign, as realism. It holds sign systems to structure and also construct reality.

I will now start to delineate Lacan's position on these issues, starting with the beginnings of semiotic theory, which goes way back into the philosophical tradition.

Mentalese

John Locke (1632–1704) introduced the formal study of signs to philosophy, and it is no coincidence that the term 'semiotics' occurs for the first time in his work. One can recapitulate Locke's philosophy of language, and that of the

British empiricists Hobbes, Berkeley, and Hume, in the view that meaning is not an independent 'thing' outside us, but primarily relates to our thinking or consciousness. Locke strikingly formulates this in his *Essay Concerning Human Understanding* (1690), where he states that 'the use of words is to be sensible marks of ideas; and the ideas they stand for are their proper and immediate signification'.[11] In the current philosophy of language, we call this 'mentalese'. The 'mentalese' tradition in the philosophy of language locates meaning in consciousness and not in the things themselves (direct reference) or in some other ontological domain (Platonism).

Beyond British empiricism we find a classical version of 'mentalese' thought in the Continental rationalism of Descartes, Leibniz, and the school of Port-Royal – a group of grammarians from seventeenth-century France (Port-Royal) that was interested in the idea of universal grammar. This rationalistic version holds ideas as present ('innate') in our consciousness from the beginning.[12] Ideas are not based on sensory perception as in the empiricist version. This rationalistic tradition makes itself felt in modern forms of 'mentalese', such as the linguistic theories of Noam Chomsky. He holds consciousness to a large extent as pre-structured: the principles of a universal grammar are 'innate'. Jerry Fodor's cognitive psychology uses the computational paradigm that considers mental processes as following strict rules in order to advance the thesis of an 'innate' 'Language of Thought'. In the glossary of his book, *The Language Instinct*, Steven Pinker defines 'mentalese' as follows: 'The hypothetical language of thought, or representation of concepts and propositions in the brain, in which ideas, including the meanings of words and sentences, are couched' (Pinker 1994).

Notwithstanding its mental character, this 'mentalese' tradition still considers meaning to be an *object*: an object in the mind. Meaning is a 'thing' that exists prior to its articulation in language. With that it fits our pre-theoretical intuitions of successful communication consisting of the correct understanding by the listener of a thought in the mind of the sender (the 'conduit metaphor' is used for this kind of communication). Communication would thus be a matter of 'coding' a thought into language and subsequently 'decoding' it.[13]

Sign and system

The work of Ferdinand de Saussure (1857–1913) radicalizes the modern turn to the thinking subject. For Saussure, one cannot conceive meaning independently of its articulation in language. The sign does not have a one-to-one relationship with its referent, and meaning is no longer the description of this reference. The concept of the sign breaks into two parts: the signifier (the acoustic image) and the signified (the concept that goes with the signifier). The sign results from the association of signifier and signified (Saussure 1916/1983: 67).

> A linguistic sign is not a link between a thing and a name, but between a concept and a sound pattern. The sound pattern is not actually a sound; for a sound is something physical. A sound pattern is the hearer's psychological impression of a sound, as given to him by the evidence of his senses. This sound pattern may be called a 'material' element only in that it is the representation of our sensory impressions. The sound pattern may thus be distinguished from the other element associated with it in a linguistic sign. This other element is generally of a more abstract kind: the concept.
>
> (Saussure 1916/1983: 66)

The 'hearer's psychological impression of a sound' creates the concept. Therefore, both the signifier and the signified are purely 'psychological' (Saussure 1916/1983: 12, 14–15, 66).[14]

Saussure's linguistic theories loosen the sign from its stable meaning. Two key views are decisive for this dissolution of the traditional sign. The first, which for Saussure is the first principle of language, is the *arbitrary nature of the sign* (Saussure 1916/1983: 67). Or, to be more specific, the arbitrariness of the link between the signifier and the signified. There is no necessary, intrinsic, direct or inevitable relationship between the signifier and the signified. Horses could just as well be called bikes. Signification – what is signified by a signifier – has an arbitrary and conventional character, and is determined by social or cultural contexts. Although Saussure mentions certain degrees of arbitrariness, the (philosophical) implication is the non-fixed character of signification. The signifier does not refer to a fixed concept. 'If words had the job of representing concepts fixed in advance, one would be able to find exact equivalents for them as between one language and another. But this is not the case' (Saussure 1916/1983: 114–115).

The *relations* between the sign and other signs within the system as a whole determine the *value* of the sign. This is the second key argument for the dissolution of the sign.

> The notion of value . . . shows us that it is a great mistake to consider a sign as nothing more than the combination of a certain sound and a certain concept. To think of a sign as nothing more would be to isolate it from the system to which it belongs. It would be to suppose that a start could be made with individual signs, and a system constructed by putting them together. On the contrary, the system as a united whole is the starting point, from which it becomes possible, by a process of analysis, to identify its constituent elements.
>
> (Saussure 1916/1983: 112)

Saussure 'decentres' the individual sign (as Lacan later on uses Saussure's work to decentre the individual person). Both the signifier and the signified are relational entities. A sound ('a') does not mean anything without its relations to other sounds ('pa'). Saussure has a special interest in language as a system ('langue'), in the system of rules and conventions that determine its personal use ('parole'). The 'embeddings' of sounds in a system of rules determines signification. By defining signs in terms of their relationship to other signs, the conception of meaning becomes purely structural and relational rather than referential. The contextual structures and rules of the semiotic system determine meaning.

Lacan's sequel to Saussure

The priority of the structural system makes the meaning of a sign determinable by analysing the underlying structures of its use. This is the appealing idea that Levi-Strauss uses for anthropology and Lacan for psychoanalysis to understand the 'deeper' meaning of the phenomena they investigate. Lacan is first of all interested in the use of Saussure's structural analysis of signs for psychoanalysis (like what the words of an analysand tell us about a patient's family structure and about his or her position in this system). In his reading of Saussure, Lacan nevertheless attempts to alter Saussure's theory on the arbitrary relationship of signifier and signified. Lacan declares the 'primacy of the signifier': the signifier determines the signified, and not the other way around. Arbitrariness then means that the 'effects of signification' (*effets de signifié*) have the appearance of having nothing to do with what causes them (Lacan 1999: 23). The signifier is first; the signified is only its *effect*. Therefore, the signified inevitably 'slips beneath' the signifier, resisting our attempts to delimit it. However, he does think that there are some 'anchoring points' (*points de capiton*, translated by Fink as 'button ties') 'by which the signifier stops the otherwise indefinite sliding of signification' (Lacan 2006: 681). Those 'points' (temporarily) establish a 'tie' between signifier and signified and thus institute some sort of stable signification – an idea strongly opposed by Derrida.[15]

Lacan's work evolves. His teachings of the 1960s and 1970s question the structuralist primacy of the relational system. His work goes beyond the analysis of hidden but more or less 'stable' significations that are laid down by the symbolic orders that language imposes. It does so in a difficult way, of which I shall try to provide an indication. Knowing that Lacan's ideas about the role of signifiers should be seen in the context of the Freudian discovery that the unconscious does not know of reference to reality, his interest in the 'free play' of the signifier can become comprehensible. Lévi-Strauss and Roland Barthes develop the concept of 'floating signifiers' to designate signifiers that are to a large extent determined by their interpreters: they mean what someone wants them to mean. They are so open to interpretation that they constitute a 'floating chain of signifieds' (Barthes 1977a: 39). Additionally, an 'empty signifier' is entirely devoid of a definite signified. Lacan also uses the notion of the floating signifier. He even glorifies Lewis Carroll's Humpty Dumpty, who reasons, 'when *I* use a word, it means just what I choose it to mean – neither more nor less'. It brings Humpty Dumpty very close to a sort of 'psychotic freedom' in which the subject does not care a straw for conventions.

Lacan also focuses on specific performances or practices that are merely instances of the use of the language system. An element of non-sense, not explicable by its relationships or its reference, 'works' in the constitution of meaning. For instance, in a ritual of ragging the rag fresher must say or do 'stupid things'. The meaning of such specific and crazy performance of language is not interpretable by its relationships towards other sounds, or by its inherent reference. But it is not without relation to meaning at all. In a paradoxical way, this 'meaningless' utterance establishes or founds the identity of the novices. Such a sign is not (fully) definable negatively, in a Saussurian way, by their contrast with other items. They are not 'whatever the others are not' (Saussure 1916/1983: 115). They also 'are what they are'. Such 'signs without meaning' are, at the most, understandable as part of a 'system' of *(identifying) marks* or signs that establish a specific lifestyle.

Lacan's thinking steers us towards a thinking of how symbolic orders are reconstructed, as in lifestyles. Not everything is understandable from the notion of structure, repression, and of 'hidden meaning'. The current, 'postmodern' context may need new categories to be adequately thought (as in Lacan's invention of the concept *sinthome*; see the end of Chapter 5). Not just the study of language puts us on the right track; it must be carried forward with an analysis of the role of 'the imagination'.[16]

2

'IMAGINATION' AS MEDIUM

2.1 The medium in between

Fantasy between perception and understanding

The word fantasy ('Phantasie', 'fantasme') derives from the Greek words 'phantasma' and 'phantasia': *appearance*. In Latin, 'phantasma' became 'fantom'. In the philosophy of Plato, 'phantasia' mostly has this meaning of appearance (Camassa 1989: 515). In his *Republic*, Plato links 'phantasia' to the concept of mimesis. At the height of ancient Greek culture, mimesis had a broad range of meanings: imitation, copying, reproducing, but also portraying, depicting, representing, and producing. In the *Republic*, Plato states that the painter copies (false) appearances and not the true world; hence, his work is necessarily false. He produces, what Plato later calls in his *Philebus*, a 'phantasma': a bad copy that only appears as a likeness to the 'real thing'. The good copy (the 'eikon') on the other side truly participates in the Idea of the thing: it approaches the ideal (cf. Doel and Clarke 1999: 277).

In his *Sophist*, Plato distinguishes explicitly between the two forms of mimesis. The one form imitates the invariable model faithfully and can therefore be called a true copy or true representation. The other form produces a deceiving likeness and is therefore false. Although Plato is ambivalent with regard to the truth-value of mimesis, in general mimesis has a somewhat pejorative meaning in his thinking: it refers to something that is not true. The same goes for fantasy. As he situates 'appearances' in the *Sophist* as a mixture of perception and opinion ('doxa'), it still belongs to an inferior understanding of the world, for it does not belong to the order of pure thinking that can offer true insight into the unchanging forms of the eternal world.

Aristotle defines 'phantasia' (provisionally) as a capacity to produce images without an actual affection of the senses: for there also appear images when the eyes are shut. Fantasy takes us beyond the actual sight of sense perception. For Aristotle, as well as for Plato, 'phantasia' as a capacity of the soul is ambivalent with regards to truth (Camassa 1989: 517). But the two agree for opposite reasons. Contrary to Plato, Aristotle considers sense perception the starting point for truth, whereas thinking may be false. 'Phantasia' as what is in between these two instances can go either way as far as its truth is concerned. Aristotle defines phantasia most prominently in *De Anima* III.3: 'phantasia is that in virtue of which we say that a phantasma [an appearance] occurs to us' (Aristotle, trans. 1986: 428a1). Especially in his *De Anima*, Aristotle understands 'phantasia' as the cause of appearance. As such a productive capacity, 'phantasia' creates conceptions ('phantasma') in the process of thinking. 'Phantasia is therefore the condition for thought in so far as it alone can present to thought the object as sensible without matter' (Castoriadis 1997: 231). In the process of remembering, it creates mental pictures ('eikon'). And in sleep it produces dream-images ('eidolon', 'phantasma'). Furthermore, it establishes ideas that function as motivating goals for human action or for movements of organisms (and is a faculty that excites or enthuses living entities). Fantasy, for Aristotle, thus occupies a central role in human existence: it is the *cause of appearance*.[1]

In Aristotle's thought, 'phantasia' occupies an *intermediate* position between sense perception and the intellect. This feature has since become a classical notion in the understanding of fantasy. It found its way into the philosophy of Aquinas, who accepted it as self-evident in his commentary on *De Anima*, via Renaissance philosophers Ficino and Pico della Mirandola to the work of Kant. To get a closer look at this fundamental role of fantasy in human reality, I will extrapolate the discussion of fantasy to this pivotal thinker of Western modernity.

The philosophical work of Immanuel Kant (1724–1804) attributes a *transcendental* role to the imagination.[2] With Kant's thinking, it is impossible to go beyond the formations that the imagination imposes upon our perception of things. We never perceive the things as they 'are in themselves' but merely as the 'appear to us'. The imagination produces reality (I will elaborate this issue later in the chapter). The (Kantian) equation of 'phantasia' with the meaning of (productive) imagination, which is nowadays current, is historically nevertheless not the first time this has happened. It was Philostratus (170–244/249 AD), one of the leading sophists or orators of his time, who, with his famous comparison between 'phantasia' and mimesis, stands at the threshold of our common conception of fantasy. He holds 'phantasia' for a wiser artist than imitation that only reproduces what it has seen ('reproductive imagination'). For 'phantasia' produces also what it has not seen, and posits it as a substitution for reality (cf. Camassa 1989: 521).[3]

The productive imagination and the unconscious

The effect of the 'unconscious productive imagination' on representation is a difficult one. The conventional reading of Aristotle's analysis of fantasy in *De Anima* testifies to this: it leaves the issue consistently out. In this reading, Aristotle's analysis of 'phantasia' tends to ignore the moment of the 'productivity' as an uncontrollable change of the representations, and solely illuminates its constitutive function in knowledge-acquisition (Camassa 1989: 519).[4]

The 'twist in representation' may be a matter of defectiveness: a flaw in our capabilities for remembering, or a neurological deficiency, so that the imagination fills in the cognitive gap between reality and mental representation. However, the gap may also be structural. Then the 'imagination', filling in the gap, is also 'productive'. It is this notion of structural inadequacy between things and their representation that rallies Kantian philosophy and psychoanalysis. The imagination is essentially 'productive' and spontaneous; there is no pure or clear reproduction of earlier perceptions (Kunz 1946: 64–65). In his text 'The Unconscious', Freud refers to Kant to emphasize the constitutive function of subjectivity in perception: 'Kant warned us not to overlook the fact that our perceptions are subjectively conditioned and must not be regarded as identical with what is perceived' (Freud 1915b: 171).

Both Kantian and Freudian theory situate the 'productive' role of the imagination in the unconscious. Already Kant emphasized the 'unconscious' aspect of imagination. This aspect is obviously present in the poetic or productive imagination: the artist creates what is not there in reality. But the question is whether it is not also 'working' in the reproductive imagination that forms our memory or recollection. Kant seems to give an affirmative answer to this: the subject cannot recollect anything without integrating it within the mind's horizon of space and time. The imagination has a *transcendental* function.

'Phantasie', 'fantasme': beyond a psychology of the imagination

In the previous paragraphs, both the words 'imagination' and 'fantasy' were used. Freud uses the term 'Phantasie' (fantasy). Kant uses the philosophical term 'Einbildungskraft' (faculty of the imagination), as he is especially interested in the 'imagination' as providing conditions of experience, where 'fantasy' would refer to the wilful or accidental. To avoid too much confusion, it must be articulated why I use the word 'fantasy' in this text.

'Fantasy' is the regular translation of the German word 'Phantasie', the one word that Freud uses in his texts. 'Phantasie' brings together two significations. 'Phantasie' designates both the *faculty* of imagination ('Einbildungskraft'), *and* the mental images or psychical representations ('Vorstellungen') that are the *product* of this imaginative power. These are also the two important significations of the word 'fantasy' in English: it is 'the faculty or activity of imagining impossible or improbable things', as well as 'a fanciful mental image, typically one on which a person often dwells and which reflects their conscious or unconscious wishes'. Besides, it has the pejorative meaning of 'an idea with no basis in reality'.

The French language discriminates between 'fantasme' and 'fantaisie'. Freud's first translators in French, Marie Bonaparte and Édouard Pichon, translate 'Phantasie' as 'fantasme' (and not 'fantaisie') to stress the conceptual importance of the fantasy-formations that the German word 'Phantasie' expresses, as distinguished from the fantasy-images (Freud's 'Phantasievorstellung'). They try not to coincide the meaning of 'Phantasie' with that of 'fantaisie' as an imaginary image. In their *Vocabulary of Psychoanalysis*, Lacan's students Jean Laplanche and Jean-Bertrand Pontalis also use 'fantasme' to translate 'Phantasie', but note that it has a narrower meaning than the German word as it would designate in particular imaginary formations and not the imaginative activity in general. Daniel Lagache, one of their former teachers and the 'editor' of their *Vocabulary* (see Roudinesco 1990: 222), therefore suggested using the ancient term 'fantaisie', as it covers both the creative activity and its productions. Following Lagache, the term 'fantaisie' came to refer to imaginary conscious or preconscious creations, without ignoring their continuity with the unconscious fantasies they reflect (Perron 2006b).

Nevertheless, the word 'fantaisie' still suggests capriciousness or gratuitousness and a lack of seriousness (Laplanche and Pontalis 1998: 152).[5] This pejorative meaning of 'fantaisie' is also the reason why Lacan most often uses the word 'fantasme' to refer to Freud's 'Phantasie'. He seems to follow a general idea in French psychoanalytic theory that the term 'fantaisie' was too marked by current usage. Lacan actually draws a strong distinction between 'fantasme' and 'fantaisie'. The word 'fantasme' expresses his ideas on the fundamental role of fantasy in psychical reality. A 'fantasme' is 'an image set to work in the signifying structure' (Lacan 2006: 532). It emphasizes both the product (image) and its symbolic production (signifying structure, the Other).

So the use of the word fantasy is difficult and tricky. I use the word fantasy, the regular translation of both the German 'Phantasie' and the French 'fantasme'. Nevertheless, I use it – consistent with its use in Kantian, Freudian, and Lacanian theory – with a special interest for its transcendental and unconscious functioning. Then fantasy surpasses the dichotomy of being either the faculty of image-production, or a product of mental activity (as such a 'fantaisie', daydreaming, or imaginary compensation – I will describe it as merely functioning in the imaginary domain). The problems of translation raise a fundamental issue, which is that psychoanalysis does not make a strict distinction between fantasy as a faculty to produce images, and the images that result from it.

What is at stake in a psychoanalytical approach of fantasy is that one cannot dissociate the act from the product. Psychoanalysis *of fantasy* cannot isolate the product 'fantasy' from the imaginative 'faculty' – this is exactly what distinguishes it from a psychology of the imagination that wants to study the product 'fantasy' by itself (Assoun 2007: 6–7). This impossibility is decisive for the problem of the unconscious. Fantasy is neither in the product (object) nor in the act of imagining (subject). It is in the intricate connection of subject and object of desire. It is their *interface*, the surface where subject and object meets. Lacan expresses this in his formula of fantasy $\$ \lozenge a$ (which can be read as: subject / window / object). Fantasy is like a window both *connecting and separating* inside and outside.

Fantasy is at the heart of our subjectivity so that the classical dichotomy of reality and illusion is too narrow for its comprehension; an opposition antedating psychoanalysis by many centuries, but probably too restrictive both to psychoanalytic theory and practice (Laplanche and Pontalis 1986: 6). To see this, we must discuss how 'Phantasie' provides the *coordinates of our reality*, both in the domain of cognition (Kant) or that of affection (Freud). That is, we must discuss it in its *transcendental* function.

2.2 Kant

The transcendental imagination

Kant's epistemology distinguishes three different levels of the relationship between the subject and its object for knowledge. First, *sensations* relate us to the object as 'Ding-an-sich' ('thing-in-itself'). 'Ding-an-sich' translates as a latter something or thinghood, a metaphysical substance: there must be something rather than nothing for sensations to occur. Second, *appearances* occur when the transcendental imagination puts the sensations of 'things' in the form of space and time, thus providing an object of experience ('Gegenstand'). Before turning to the third level of knowledge, provided by the understanding, I will discuss this operation of the imagination in more detail.

In his *Anthropology from a Pragmatic Point of View*, Kant differentiates 'phantasia' (that is here equivalent to 'Einbildungskraft', imagination) into a 'faculty of the original representation of the object (exhibition originaria)'; that is to say preceding the perception of the object, and 'a faculty of the derived representation (exhibition derivative), which recalls to mind a previous empirical perception' (Kant 1798/1974: §28). In his *Critique of Pure Reason*, Kant analyses this difference between a productive and a reproductive imagination as the difference between a transcendental and an empirical imagination.

Kant's philosophy considers the spatio-temporal world as a setting ('Setzung') that we as subjects of knowledge continuously execute. To be apprehensible, the manifold empirical sensations (the *matter* of our knowledge) must necessarily be put into the *form* of space and time. Things can only appear to us within the horizon of the time–space dimension. This synthesizing of sensations into appearances is an activity of the *transcendental imagination*, an *a priori* structure of the human mind that precedes sensibility and hence conditions our perception. It synthesizes the manifold sense-impressions by putting them in the dimensions of space and time – like a television synthesizes the signals by putting them successively and spatially on the screen. The transcendental imagination introduces unity into sensations – as a manifold of troubling sensations gets certain coherence by putting them, for instance, within a specific framework of a family history.[6]

Kant describes the synthesis in general as 'the mere effect of the imagination, of a blind though indispensable function of the soul, without which we would have no cognition at all, but of which we are seldom even conscious' (Kant 1789/1996: A 78).[7] We do not willingly execute this (synthesizing) activity of the imagination. It is, on the other hand, something preceding the reflexive self which is the condition of possibility of cognition. 'The principle of the necessary unity of the pure (productive) synthesis of the imagination prior to apperception is thus the ground of the possibility of all cognition, especially that of experience' (Kant 1789/1996: A 118).

This brings us to the third 'relation to the object', the cognitive one. According to Kant, 'innate' concepts or categories of the understanding make appearances into an object for knowledge ('Objekt'): 'Appearances, so far as they are thought as objects according to the unity of the categories, are called *phaenomena*' (Kant 1789/1996: A 249). The understanding connects the appearances into coherent, knowable objects ('phaenomena').

To understand how the understanding works, we must take a look at its categories and schemes. Then again the central role of the imagination will become clear.

Schematism as the 'hidden art' in the depths of the human soul

The human mind connects or combines appearances to make sense of them. This, Kant says, is an activity of the understanding. The understanding relates the appearances to an object according to certain concepts. For Kant, coherent perception is impossible without concepts of understanding, or categories. A concept is an idea (in Greek: 'phantasia', 'phantasma') of the understanding through which the human mind understands phenomena as a meaningful unity. Understanding consists of successfully combining appearances by means of concepts.

The unifying qualities of the categories turn the diversity of appearances into a coherent object of knowledge. So, although many things may appear as objects – 'Gegenstände' – in which I can throw away my trash, I (must) understand that only some of them are a dustbin. The question is how to apply a concept correctly to an empirical appearance. For Kant, this application occurs according to certain schemes that mediate empirical reality and the intellectual concept. A correct use of concepts requires some sort of 'intermediaries' that connect ('interface') empirical reality and concepts, the sensible and the intellectual domain. Kant calls them 'schemes'.[8]

The scheme is a rule according to which the imagination synthesizes intuitions ('Anschauungen') and thus 'prepares' them for understanding. The most general rule is that of the sequence: we always experience things in time consecutively. Therefore, it may not surprise us that time is the primary scheme: 'Time is the *a priori* formal condition of all appearances in general' (Kant 1789/1996: A 34). Time is the form of the inner intuition. Space is the form of all outer intuitions: when we perceive something outside us, it is in space. However, for Kant, space already belongs to the inner state: whether a representation corresponds to an object in outer reality or not, it is basically a representation of an inner intuition that has time as its form. The schemata that structure and organize our coherent understanding of things 'are therefore nothing but *a priori* time-determinations in accordance with rules' (Kant 1789/1996: A 145). Heidegger adds to this: 'The schemata of pure concepts of understanding, the categories, are *a priori* time-determinations and as such they are a transcendental product of the pure power of imagination' (Heidegger 1997: 292). Schemes are about a 'logical' determination of time. In the *Critique of Pure Reason*, causality is therefore the most important concept of the understanding.[9]

I will try to illustrate this. Each time that I type on my keyboard (A) and see sentences appear on the screen (B) I come to connect A and B as cause and effect. The fact that B occurs each time after A (which is not exactly the same as B because of A) is what Kant calls the *scheme* of the concept causality. Schemes aim at 'the unity in the determination of sensibility' (Kant 1789/1996: A 140) and are employed by the imagination to 'draw' the figure of a concept: 'the schema of sensible concepts (such as figures in space) is a product and as it were a monogram of pure *a priori* imagination, through which and in accordance with which the images first become possible' (Kant 1789/1996: A 141–142). The understanding subsequently puts the connection of causality into the material, or it includes it under the concept of causality. As this concept is not derived from empirical perception, Kant comes to see this concept as one of the twelve categories of the understanding, that is to say the fundamental concepts that have their origin purely, *a priori*, in the understanding itself. Kant's answer to the question why the categories would be applicable to the material of perception in the first place is that the understanding does not take its fundamental concepts from empirical reality, but *puts them in it*. The spatio-temporal appearances therefore already contain the schemes. His epistemology is idealistic in the sense that the understanding (also) constructs its objects.[10]

Kant gives the example of the concept of a dog:

> The concept of a dog signifies a rule in accordance with which my imagination can specify the shape of a four-footed animal in general, without being restricted to any single particular shape that experience offers me or any possible image that I can exhibit *in concreto*. This schematism of our understanding with regard to appearances and their mere form is a hidden art in the depths of the human soul.
>
> (Kant 1789/1996: A 141)[11]

2.3 Freud

Fantasy within the limits of the pleasure principle

Although it is nearly impossible to make a clear demarcation among Freud's different uses of the notion 'fantasy' – which, consequently, I will not do – it is clear that Freud uses fantasy first of all as what we would call 'fantasizing' ('Phantasieren'). Fantasy, then, is the hallucinatory fulfilment of wishes that cannot be satisfied in 'real life'. The paradigmatic example of this kind of fantasy is the daydream, a (pre)conscious reverie intended to provide some sort of imaginary satisfaction. In 'Hysterical Phantasies and their Relation to Bisexuality', Freud writes: 'These phantasies are satisfactions of wishes proceeding from deprivation and longing' (Freud 1908: 159). Freud finds that these fantasies often originate in infantile experience, which led him to his theory of auto-eroticism.

Freud discovers that in the first stages of the development of the drive (oral, anal), it finds satisfaction in its own body. When a child sucks on its thumb, for instance, it repeats the (oral) pleasure of sucking on the breast that originally went along with the taking in of food.[12] This auto-eroticism functions according to the pleasure principle governing the most 'primitive' processes in the psychic system that Freud therefore calls primary processes, wherein energy floats freely, with no 'regulation' by the laws that govern social reality (see also Chapter 1, §1.2). The pleasure principle supplies the only rule: to avoid displeasure or, when the tension is too high, to gain pleasure through a discharge of energy. Hallucinating the object is the fastest way to (re)gain satisfaction. For the primary processes it is of no interest that this is an 'imaginary shortcut' towards a satisfying object (it does not care about the laws of outer reality). All it cares about is that the object is *perceived* as being satisfactory. It only focuses on an 'identity in perception' ('Wahrnehmungsidentität').[13]

In *The Interpretation of Dreams*, Freud describes this primitive functioning of the psychical apparatus as follows:

> we were already able to add a second hypothesis, to the effect that the accumulation of excitation . . . is felt as unpleasure and that it sets the apparatus in action with a view to repeating the experience of satisfaction, which involved a diminution of excitation and was felt as pleasure. A current of this kind in the apparatus, starting from unpleasure and aiming at pleasure, we have termed a 'wish' . . . The first wishing seems to have been a hallucinatory cathecting of the memory of satisfaction.
>
> (Freud 1900: 598)

In 'Formulations on the Two Principles of Mental Functioning', Freud comes closest to a formal definition of fantasy. Here he connects fantasy explicitly to the pleasure principle. Fantasy then is a (auto-erotic) retrieving – or retracing – of pleasure by means of a hallucination of the object of the wish.

> A general tendency of our mental apparatus, which can be traced back to the economic principle of saving expenditure (of energy), seems to find expression in the tenacity with which we hold on to the sources of pleasure at our disposal, and in the difficulty with which we renounce them. With the introduction of the reality principle one species of thought-activity was split off; it was kept free from reality-testing and remained subordinated to the pleasure principle alone.[14] This activity is *phantasying*, which begins already in children's play, and later, continued as *day-dreaming*, abandons dependence on real objects.
>
> (Freud 1911: 222)

Freud considers a specific relationship between fantasy and sexuality. Sexuality, a broad notion, contains all activities that generate in one way or another pleasurable feeling in one of the erogenous zones of the body. Freud discovered that the 'sexual' drive is made up of different partial drives that centre on erogenous zones (mouth, anus, even the eye). This allows him to formulate in 'Three Essays on the Theory of Sexuality' (1905) his 'scandalous' theory of infantile sexuality. Nevertheless, we must stress here that this 'sexuality' of the partial drives is not equal to what we normally consider sexuality (i.e. genital sexuality), which, according to Freud, only becomes dominant with puberty.

As the sexual drive could long-lastingly find satisfaction in its own body, and was thus not subjected to the reality principle, the field was open to the fantasies that accompanied it. Since the sexual drive must also – although with delay – find its object in the external world for the subject to stay healthy, those fantasies are particularly vulnerable to repression: they may be impossible in the socialized world, or become unacceptable for the subject. When, in the case of the masturbatory act, 'the subject renounces this type of satisfaction, composed of masturbation and phantasy, the action is given up, while the phantasy, from being conscious, becomes unconscious' (Freud 1908: 161). Sexual fantasies play a central role in mental life, despite – or rather, because of – the fact that they in particular meet the fate of repression, which is why Freud calls them 'the weak spot in our psychical organization' (Freud 1911: 223). This repression creates the psychic disposition towards neurosis in man, the conflict between unconscious desires and conscious control.

Unconscious fantasy

Some commentators tend to assign a 'central usage' of fantasy in Freud's work (Bott Spillius 2001: 361). This 'central usage' would be fantasy within the limits of the pleasure principle, as an imaginary representation that does not take into account the demands and constraints that reality imposes upon us. Fantasy then functions as the pivotal notion for distinguishing reality from illusion. Freud (1911) may have contributed to the misleading idea of contrasting imagination with reality by connecting in 'Formulations on the Two Principles of Mental Functioning' fantasy explicitly to the pleasure principle (see Modell 2006: 107).

It is therefore not surprising that during the *Controversial Discussions* in the British Psycho-Analytical Society in the 1940s, Anna Freud adopts this usage. She places a strong emphasis on the role of the ego in her father's conceptualization of the mind as consisting of Id, Ego, and Superego. Her work is later to be followed by that of the ego-psychologists (with Heinz Hartmann, Ernst Kris, and Rudolf Loewenstein as its chief proponents), who focus on the integrative and organizing functions of the ego and thus develop the adaptive point of view that presupposes a concordance between man's inner world and his surrounding world. Contrary to ego-psychology, the French stream in psychoanalysis does not interpret Freud's work as an adaptive model but as a conflictual one: not just the ego but above all the (subversive) subject of desire is central to subjectivity. Then a clear demarcation of reality and illusion is rather problematic. Fantasy is not just a 'reserve' kept free from reality testing; there is also the 'productive' function of fantasy.[15]

The controversy shows that a crucial issue in a theory of fantasy is that of consciousness. Are we *consciously aware* that our use of fantasy leads us into an imaginary world that we can distinguish from reality? This is the model of daydreaming, as a product of the ego that tries to compensate for its (imagined) shortcomings. Or is the indulging in fantasies also, or to a large extent, an unconscious activity? And how sharp is the distinction between unconscious and conscious fantasies? For although there is clearly a difference between the fantasy-work in dreams and in daydreams, even the material of daydreams stems from the unconscious. The question of consciousness and the unconscious with regards to fantasy was therefore also a central issue of the *Controversial Discussions* (Bott Spillius 2001).

In her paper 'The Nature and Function of Phantasy', which was first given at the *Discussions*, Susan Isaacs departs from the central role of unconscious fantasies in the work of Melanie Klein to introduce a distinction between conscious and unconscious fantasies. She suggests the graphological use of *ph*antasies for unconscious fantasies, and *f*antasies for conscious ones. Since then the Kleinian school in psychoanalysis – which focuses on the 'unconscious all along' aspect of fantasy: it is an activity that accompanies all mental activity – uses this difference between *f*antasy and *ph*antasy to stress its conscious or unconscious character. As this issue touches upon the theoretical core of psychoanalysis, it may not surprise that it has evoked a lot of discussion ever since.

Jean Laplanche and Jean-Bertrand Pontalis consider it a superficial distinction that does not do justice to the complexity of Freud's thought. Furthermore, in the translations of Freud's work, the double use of terms for the one term 'Phantasie' leads to arbitrary interpretations (Laplanche and Pontalis 1998: 156). Although they acknowledge the development in Freud's metapsychological status of fantasy, this does not suppress the homology between the different levels of fantasy. Conscious fantasies may have a root in unconscious fantasies, and one may be able to 'work through' unconscious fantasies and so become aware of them. However, when one wants to distinguish fantasy, one must not use the barrier between the (pre)conscious and the unconscious system, Laplanche and Pontalis state, but one must discriminate within the unconscious itself: have the fantasies been unconscious all along or have they been forgotten and repressed? (Laplanche and Pontalis 1986: 21–22).

The mind-bending issue of psychoanalysis is the distinction between fantasies that constitute (authentic) desire and those that deceive it; between fantasy as a *necessary function or medium*, and as an *arbitrary deviation* (cf. Assoun 2007: 93–94). This issue expresses itself in many crucial questions. Can a final distinction between authenticity and seduction ever be drawn? What is my true Self? Can we say what is real, or what we really want? What is healthiness? Can one conclude an analysis – and is a conclusion a matter of truth, or of force, power, money, authority, tiredness, coincidence, ritualism . . .?[16]

A schematism of desire?

In 'From the History of an Infantile Neurosis' (the 'Wolf Man'), Freud states:

> the phylogentically inherited schemata, which, like the categories of philosophy, are concerned with the business of 'placing' the impressions derived from actual experience. I am inclined to take the view that they are precipitates from the history of human civilization. The Oedipus complex, which comprises a child's relation to his parents, is one of them – is, in fact, the best known member of the class. Wherever experiences fail to fit in with the hereditary schema, they become remodelled in the imagination . . . We are often able to see the schema triumphing over the experience of the individual.
>
> (Freud 1918: 119)

Thus Freud formulates his controversial 'phylogenetic' hypothesis, which seeks to explain the general structure of primal fantasies and of the Oedipus complex. Individual development (onto-genesis) would follow the process of human evolution (phylo-genesis). 'Impressive analogies from biology have prepared us to find that the individual's mental development repeats the course of human development in an abbreviated form' (Freud 1910: 97). Freud observes that there are certain (primal) fantasies that seem to characterize each person's individual development. These are the fantasies of observing sexual intercourse between the parents (the primal scene), fantasies of seduction and of castration. He finds that those fantasies have recurrent narratives and are often associated with certain psychopathological formations. He tries to analyse these fantasies first of all by using the material from the patient's individual history. As Freud concludes in his text on the Wolf Man, we may only assume a schematic (inherited) structure of desire when the interpretation of the individual biography has reached its limits. Philosophical thoughts on transcendental structures are 'only admissible when psychoanalysis strictly observes the correct order of precedence, and, after forcing its way through the strata of what has been acquired by the individual, comes at last upon traces of what has been inherited' (Freud 1918: 121). Nevertheless, he arrives at such traces to explain the recurrent structures of certain fantasies. The Oedipus complex, which structures the child's libidinal position in relation to its parents, is also not deducible from individual history. Thus Freud jumps into the 'morass' of phylogenetic explanation – and was heavily criticized for it (see Perron 2006c).

Not only does Freud believe in the development of the libido (with its possible vicissitudes) in individual life. As a confirmed evolutionist, he also thinks that the evolution of the human species lays down some specifically human structures in man's psychic constitution. Via Darwin, Lamarck (who develops the idea of the inheritance of acquired character-traits), and Haeckel (the development of an individual organism goes through the same stages as the species as a whole), he arrives at his great hypothesis of the phylogenetic origin of the Oedipus complex, as described in *Totem and Taboo* (Perron 2001: 590). The founding experiences of each individual life history actually took place at the origin of mankind. In man's prehistory, the sons killed the father of the 'primitive horde', who kept all the females for himself. The guilt and remorse that followed this primeval murder then became a universal aspect of all human beings. The Oedipus complex repeats this phylogenetic origin that provides the matrix for our desires.

Although many critical remarks on the phylogenetic explanation of fantasies are rightfully made, the interesting thing is that such an explanation puts us on the track of thinking fantasy as a structure that transcends our experience – and actually provides the conditions of experience. For what Freud states is that the 'hereditary schema' makes 'normal' experience contain a conditional element of structuring. Like the prohibition of incest (our 'condition of possibility') makes love relations within kinship a psychic impossibility. Imaginary forms of compensation result for representations that do not fit within schematized reality (so that when I do fall in love with my niece, fantasizing offers a way out of the conflict).

Schemes by which we conceptualize reality do not merely *follow* sense-impression, but actually *structure* it. With that notion of inherited schemes, Freud's thinking of fantasy seems to resemble the Kantian theory of imagination as an *a priori* condition of experience.[17]

Schemes are the 'blueprint' of our psychological self (a more current and neurobiological terminology would speak of those schemes as 'in our genes'). This is an interesting line of thought, especially for approaching the work of Lacan that considers human reality so much modelled, not by inherited biological factors, but by imaginary forms and transmissible symbolic structures.

Part II

LACAN'S THEORY OF FANTASY

3

FRAMEWORKS FOR DESIRE

3.1 Desire

Anthropology of desire

Lacan situates his theory in a long tradition of thought profoundly connecting human existence to desire. In particular, the rationalistic ethics of Baruch de Spinoza (1632–1677), a Jew excommunicated from the synagogue due to his pantheistic vision of God, interested Lacan: a diagram of Spinoza's Ethics covered his bedroom wall while he was a teenager. As it was for Spinoza, for Lacan desire is the essence of human existence (cf. Lacan 1998b: 275). Actually one must be more precise, for, Lacan says, in an a-theological system (that pulls man away from the centre of the world), the term 'man' is impossible to conserve. Then he suggests substituting Spinoza's formula that 'desire is the essence of man' by 'desire is the essence of reality' (Lacan 1966–1967, 16 November 1966).

As desire is no solid basis on which a fixed determination of man can be made, his essence is characterized as the 'non-determined animal'. It is only with the disappearance of the foundations of man (the 'death of God') that the 'homelessness' of his desire is thinkable in its radical quality. Whereas Lacan's a-theological thinking of desire seems almost impossible without the Nietzschean notion of the 'death of God', the absence of references to Nietzsche in his work are remarkable. For the 'death of God' implies not only that a metaphysical or religious fulfilment of desire is impossible, it moves every notion of a 'realization' (of desire, man, the world) into the realm of the impossible.[1]

There is a crack in the ontological homogeneity of the world, so that the metaphysical dream of completion falls apart. As it puts this rupture at the centre of man (the 'split subject'), Lacan's theory of desire has a similarity with other great thinkers about man after the 'death of god'. Heidegger characterizes man as ex-sistent, Plessner as ex-centric. Man has lost the substantial centre of his existence; it is an empty place now. Thinking the subject of desire must depart from this 'void', Žižek summarizes these insights by considering the decisive insight of modern Western thought to be that of the subject not being a steady substance but an empty core, a 'substanceless void of the pure *cogito*' (Žižek 1992: 168).

As a theory of desire, Lacanian theory distinguishes itself from three major traditions in the conception of man. *Religious anthropology* understands man – as a 'homo religiosus' – from his relations to the gods or God. It links up man's desire with a divine dimension that can salvage man's shortcomings. *Rational anthropology* puts the autonomous reason, as discovered by the ancient Greeks, on the foreground and considers it the excellent instance of the human being ('animal rationale') through which it can realize or contemplate the ideal world. So Kant states in his *Anthropology from a Pragmatic Point of View* (1798) that the process of Enlightenment can lead to a full realization of man. Not the individual person but mankind as a whole fulfils its rational nature by realizing the goals it sets itself. Other rational philosophers, such as Hegel and Schelling, articulate an anthropology in which the goal is a self-consciousness of the Spirit. *Biological anthropology* traces the essence of man back to his biological substance. Then man should be understood at the natural level, without crude opposition between man and animal (as in the rational anthropology).

Lacan's conception of man as 'desiring animal' moves away from those classical lines of thought in anthropological thinking. He openly dissociates himself from the biological model that was dominant in his days (and still is). For 'biologics' in psychoanalysis leads to an obliteration of the distinction between nature and culture, and to a confusion of desire and need, of drives and instincts. To avoid such a muddle, Lacan introduces a strong distinction between need, demand, and desire.

Need is a psychological tension that results from physiological disequilibria. Physiological processes determine the object of the need. Need is removed when it has found an adequate object: food soothes one's hunger. With *demand* we enter the cultural domain of intersubjectivity. It is the articulation of need. Through this articulation the subject directs itself not just towards objects that can satisfy its needs, but also towards the other. The demand is essentially a demand for love. The infant that expresses its needs, however inarticulately, does not solely want a satisfaction of its needs. It also demands the other's presence, a presence symbolizing its love. However, the other cannot provide the unconditional love that the subject demands. After the satisfaction of needs, something remains left.[2] The fact that the love of the other is 'not all' causes the surplus of demand that is called *desire*. 'Desire is neither the appetite for satisfaction, nor the demand for love, but the difference that results from the subtraction of the first from the second, the very phenomenon of their splitting (*Spaltung*)' (Lacan 2006: 580). The cause of desire is a split (gap) between need and love. This cause of desire is what Lacan later calls the 'objet petit a', the *object a*.

'Instincts' and fantasy

Ethnology allows us to situate fantasy in relation to the problem of the 'instinct'. It propounds that what distinguishes man from the animal is the latter's adaptation to a uniform environment. An animal inhabits the natural space of its immediate environment, and its instincts express this immediacy. For Freud, such animal instincts are not what the drive is about. The drive is on the border of the mental and the somatical, it is a psychical representation of the stimuli that come from the body and reach out into the mental. 'The whole flux of our mental life and everything that finds expression in our thoughts are derivations and representatives of the multifarious instincts [drives] that are innate in our physical constitution' (Freud 1932: 221). Man's relationship to his environment is not so natural, and one must take account of this 'breach of man out of nature' and distinguish between the *instinct* and the *drive*, to which, for instance, the work of Max Scheler testifies.[3]

Whereas the instinct has a natural object, the drive does not. It has, as one says in psychoanalysis, a psychical object. This psychical construction of 'immanent images' guides the drive in relating to images of what attracts the organism in the outside world. Those 'drive-immanent' images are what we call 'phantasms', or objects of fantasy (Kunz 1946: 125). Lacan grasps this functioning of 'phantasms' first of all by analysing the role of images in mental phenomena (such as in paranoia, which was the subject of his doctoral thesis). Psychoanalysis sets out that the image has a

> formative function in the subject, and revealed that if common images make for certain individual differences in tendencies, they do so as variations of the matrices that other specific images – which in my vocabulary correspond to antquity's term 'imago' – constitute for the 'instincts' themselves.
>
> (Lacan 2006: 85)

Images are 'matrices' for the instinct and turn it into the drive that does not have a natural but a psychical and 'cultural' object. Images are essentially connected to experiences of pleasure: they are invested with libido (so that objects of fantasy are largely working on the level of affection). The 'unnatural' phenomenon in man is that besides the instinctive striving for the fulfilment of needs, there also is a separated striving for pleasure (Kunz 1946: 107).[4]

The drive has a psychical object, and fantasy is the formation of this object. To understand how Lacan's work considers fantasy as the primary formation of the object, we must start at the beginnings and consider how in the early work of Lacan fantasy is primarily thought of as the imaginary order.

3.2 The ego of reflection

The mirror-image

Lacan's theory of the imaginary order consists first of all of a theorization of man's identification with the mirror-image. His theory of the mirror stage fills in the 'gap' in Freud's theory about the 'new psychical action' that the different partial drives need to convert from the stage of auto-eroticism, where satisfaction is gained from the individual's own body, to the stage of object-love, where the individual invests its libido (also) in others. In the intermediate stage, the ego emerges as the result of the partial drives' investment in something that gives the subject, for the first time, a unified sense of self: the self-image.

From his work 'On Narcissism: An Introduction' (1914) onward, Freud defines narcissism as an *investment of libido in the ego*. But Freud does not clarify how this investment comes about, and thus leaves open the question concerning the 'mysterious' emergence of the ego. Lacan gives an explanation by claiming that a primitive version of a unified self-experience occurs when the infant recognizes itself for the first time in the mirror. Between six and eighteen months the infant shows, by means of the illuminative mimicry of the *Aha-erlebnis*, that it recognizes the image in the mirror as itself.

> Indeed, this act, far from exhausting itself, as in the case of the monkey, in eventually acquired control over the uselessness of the image, immediately gives rise in a child to a series of gestures in which he playfully experiences the relationship between the movements made in the image and the reflected environment, and between this virtual complex and the reality it duplicates – namely, the child's own body, and the persons and even things, around him.
>
> (Lacan 2006: 75)

The ego expresses a mastery over the diverse sensations of the direct bodily awareness. It expresses this feeling of mastery or control in certain dispositions or states of mind. In the mirror stage, this is the state of mind of jubilation: the celebration of the infant in front of the mirror signals the event of controlling its own body via identification with the 'illusory' other.[5]

> The privilege of that experience is to offer the subject a virtual reality, non-realized, grasped as such: to conquer. Every possibility for human reality to construct itself passes literally through it.
>
> (Lacan 1998a: 225; my translation)

As identification with images, the ego opens up virtual space: the alter ego of (ideal) images is its constant companion. Therefore, we not only exist at the point where our own body physically is, but also at the virtual place where we imagine ourselves to be (our 'Second Self'[6]).

This order of images resembles the functioning of the imago, which Jung originally introduced in psychoanalytic theory.

> The function of the mirror stage thus turns out, in my view, to be a particular case of the function of imagos, which is to establish a relationship between an organism and its reality – or, as they say, between the *Innenwelt* and the *Umwelt*.
>
> (Lacan 2006: 78)[7]

The imago colours the way we relate to other people: we perceive the others through the lens of the various imagos. Although Lacan is largely negative in his judgement of Jung's notion of universal prototypes, also in his theory the image functions as a medium of perception; the image of the body constitutes the ego.[8]

Two narcissisms

The formative function of the mirror stage in the development of the ego shows that the 'synthetization' of the partial drives' objects into one narcissistic image is a foundational process. Therefore, narcissism is not merely something illusory that can or must be overcome, but also a 'deviation' that characterizes the human relation to the object itself. I will introduce this duplicity of the imaginary order with Lacan's discussion of 'The two narcissisms' in the tenth chapter of his first seminar held in 1953–1954.

There Lacan explains things as follows. First, there is the narcissism that constitutes the ego, and this identification with the body image allows for the fact that organisms are attracted to images of objects of the same species (the 'immanent images'):

> First of all, there is, in fact, a narcissism connected with the corporeal image. This image is identical for the entirety of the subject's mechanisms and gives his *Umwelt* its form, in as much as he is man and not horse. It makes up the unity of the subject . . . it makes possible the organization of the totality of reality into a limited number of preformed frameworks.
>
> (Lacan 1988a: 125)

The 'capture by the imago of the human form' (Lacan 2006: 92), the identification with our mirror image, makes us human and explains why we are (sexually) attracted to other humans and not to, for instance, horses.[9] The montage of the object of the partial drives functions as a 'framework' for, for instance, finding a sexual partner. This shows that there is a narcissistic element in the choice of the love-object, as Freud had already stated in his theory of narcissism. In *On Narcissism: An Introduction*, Freud thinks that a person may love, according to the narcissistic type, what he himself is (i.e. himself), or what he himself was.

> In general, man has two original sexual objects and his later life depends on the one upon which he remains fixated. These two sexual objects are, for each individual, the woman (the mother, the children's nurse, etc.) and his own person. It is a question of getting rid of both of them and not lingering over them.
>
> (Freud 1914: 90)

The drives, which are first of all auto-erotic, find a unified object in the form of the self-image (Lacan), and this narcissistic image influences our object-choice (where Freud thinks that homosexuality is also explained by a fixation on the own person as sexual object). Love is not without narcissistic components: in the other we love what we would have wanted to be, or we love another because she loves (an ideal image of) me. For Lacan, therefore, love has a 'fundamentally narcissistic structure' (Lacan 1998b: 186), as it is 'one's own ego that one loves in love, one's own ego made real on the imaginary level' (Lacan 1988a: 142).

Narcissistic identifications with others are only possible after the coming into existence of the ego by means of the identification with the body (mirror) image. Such (secondary narcissistic) identifications actually belong to the dynamic of the ego itself, as it is always looking for and anticipating forms of autonomy and control that it has not reached yet. Also others can function as such fascinating mirrors. However, these identifications with others also dismantle the autonomy of the ego. This leads to the seemingly paradoxical situation that 'I is another' (a quote Lacan uses from the poet Rimbaud; Lacan 2006: 96). It is this process that also causes the ego to be 'frustration in its essence. Not frustration of a desire of the subject, but frustration by an object in which his desire is alienated' (Lacan 1968: 11). As Lacan puts forward in his text on 'Aggressivity in Psychoanalysis', it is this objectification of the ego that accounts for a fundamental aggressivity: it leads to an aggressive rivalry with the image (the other) that the ego has turned itself into. As this image is both the self-image and the image of the other, the aggressivity can both turn itself against the self ('suicidal') and against the other. As the ego is thus constantly 'haunted' by its objectified form, it accounts for the fundamental 'paranoiac structure of the ego' (Lacan 2006: 93).

To put this in general terms: in man the relation to the environment via constitutive images of its own (bodily) form is once more deflected by the identification with images of others. While imaginary identifications can lead to all sorts of 'delusions', it is at the same time also due to these processes that for man the variances in the 'object' are so large.[10]

> For the animal there are a limited number of pre-established correspondences between its imaginary structure and whatever interests it in its *Umwelt*. In man, by contrast, the reflection in the mirror indicates an original noetic possibility, and introduces a second narcissism. Its fundamental pattern is immediately the relation to the other. For man the other has a captivating value, on account of the anticipation that is represented by the unitary image as it is perceived either in the mirror or in the entire reality of the fellow being.
>
> (Lacan 1988a: 125)

This second-order narcissism also accounts for forms of 'madness' as in amorousness: by trying to be like the ideal other. According to Lacan, one of the most fundamental notions in Freud's work concerns the possible strict equivalence between object and ego-ideal, for instance in the case of being in love (Lacan 1988a: 126). In such a realized fantasy, the other is the ideal; I am as the other, or at least I aspire to be.

An optical model of consciousness

As the following quote from *The Interpretation of Dreams* shows, Freud already used the reference to optics – not just to an optical apparatus as the telescope, but also to the microscope and the camera (Freud 1900: 536) – to give a graphic representation of the psychic apparatus.

> [I]deas, thoughts and psychical structures in general must never be regarded as localized in organic elements of the nervous system but rather, as one might say, *between* them, where resistances and facilitations [*Bahnungen*] provide the corresponding correlates. Everything that can be an object of our internal perception is *virtual*, like the image produced in a telescope by the passage of light-rays. But we are justified in assuming the existence of the systems (which are not in any way psychical entities themselves and can never be accessible to our psychical perception) like the lenses of the telescope, which cast the image. And, if we pursue this analogy, we may compare the censorship between two systems to the refraction which takes place when a ray of light passes into a new medium.
>
> (Freud 1900: 611)

Representations and thoughts are like 'virtual images' that are not located *in* organic elements of the nervous system but rather *in between* those elements, where the effects of the unconscious mould them, like the lenses shape the image in a telescope.[11]

When we consider the fundamental relation between the (development of) the ego and images, it may not surprise us that Lacan, like Freud, also uses optical models as metaphors for the functioning of the psyche. Lacan compares the organic apparatus to the mechanism of the camera; what we apprehend are the images (Lacan 1988a: 123). He considers there to be optics, when for each given point in real space, there is a corresponding point in imaginary space (Lacan 1988a: 76). Optics demonstrates the intermingling of what we are inclined to call real space (or the absolute space of Newtonian physics as supposedly being an infinite substance independent from the bodies and human subjects that inhabit it) with imaginary space. We cannot avoid decorating space with our reflected figures: 'I would say that it is the subjective possibility of the mirror projection of such a field into the other's field that gives human space its originally "geometrical structure", a structure I would willingly characterize as *kaleidoscopic*' (Lacan 2006: 99). For Lacan, the optical schema illustrates the strict intricacy in the psychic economy of the imaginary and the real (Lacan 1988a: 78).

In his second seminar, Lacan uses the camera to provide a 'materialist definition of consciousness' (Lacan 1988b: ch. 4). This definition might remind us of the modern materialistic and mechanistic explanation of physical space in which everything revolves around matter and the forces that move them, with no room for something like a soul or a mind. Lacan now explains consciousness without falling back on something like a soul or an immaterial mind. His materialist definition considers consciousness an *effect* of reflection, of our relation to images, an effect that takes place at the surface. It considers that

> all sorts of things can behave like mirrors. All that's needed is that the conditions be such that to one point of a reality there should correspond an effect at another point, that a bi-univocal correspondence occurs between two points in real space.
>
> (Lacan 1988b: 49)

In the metaphoric of optics, consciousness is an effect of reflection.

When consciousness is like the images captured by a camera, it is already mediated by the 'apparatus'. To understand this 'apparatus', we now must discuss the signifying dimension of the images. It is because of this symbolic dimension of images that fantasy is not deducible to the imaginary order. Fantasy is an 'image set to work in a signifying chain'.[12]

3.3 The subject of the unconscious

Alienation

For Lacan, to exist is to live within the domain of the Other. The concept of the Other originates in the simple fact that speaking supposes another person that the word is addressed to. So the first Other is the mother, the parents or guardians. In Lacanian theory, one writes the Other with a capital 'O' to indicate its general meaning as the *place* to which the word addresses itself – which is not necessarily another concrete person. Lacan's notion of the Other does not only refer to Freud's 'other scene' as the unconscious representation in the psychical apparatus of the drives, but simultaneously to the dimension of language. The Other is the locus wherein speaking and truthfulness take place. 'The Other is the locus in which is situated the chain of signifiers that governs whatever may be made present of the subject – it is the field of that living being in which the subject has to appear' (Lacan 1998b: 203). It is obviously not the reservoir of libido that is the Id in Freud's theory, but a reservoir of signifying elements. Actually, the energetic field of the libido is steered by these signifying elements (like one specific signifying element, a word, a look, a garment can arouse our desire).

The discourse of the unconscious is for Lacan basically a linguistic discourse. Our use of language constitutes the symbolic subject of the unconscious (cf. Lacan 1998b: ch. 16). Subjectivity is basically linguistic intersubjectivity: human beings cannot come into existence as subjects of desire but through the signifying function of language. Our use of language and our desire go hand in hand: they create the human being as a compound substance. As our subjectivity ('inside') is so much connected to the realm of language ('outside'), we are necessarily alienated. The original 'substitution through the signifier' implies that we are alienated from the beginning.

In the first phase of his thinking, until the end of the 1950s, Lacan focuses on the concept of *alienation*.[13] The multivalent notion that 'desire is the desire of the Other' summarizes this tendency. This means first of all that man *desires to be the object of the desire of the other*. Via Kojève this leads back to the Hegelian notion of recognition as a fulfilment of desire. It also means that the subject *desires as another*. The desire of others mediates our desire: I want something because someone else wants it. In addition to this, it implies that desire is a *desire for the other*, as in Plato's conception of Eros, with the added 'sexual' dimension that desire is thought of having in psychoanalysis. Lastly, it means that desire is always 'the *desire for something else*' (Lacan 2006: 431).[14]

The early Lacan follows the Hegelian tradition in the analysis of desire. At the apogee of his structuralist period, as in his first seminars at the beginning of the 1950s, he seems to believe in a full determination by the symbolic Other. Symbolic laws govern the reality of man, who can only find some sort of freedom by recognizing the law. It is the (structural) field of the Other that determines meaning. One could illustrate the workings of the realm of the Other using Orson Welles' radio transmission of 30 October 1938: *The War of the Worlds*. Many listeners actually experienced this 'news-broadcast' as being the commentary of earth's invasion by Martians. They were lured because the institutional contexts of Hollywood and of radio-news were changed without any (explicit) notice to the listener. This shows that for something to be experienced as *true*, it is necessary that one *believes* in the whole network of cultural, institutional, and professional conventions that present it. For if this act of faith was not (unconsciously) executed (that is, when it was made explicit that the broadcast was a Hollywood production), all the commotion about being attacked by Martians would not have occurred. It is precisely the act of belief in the context in which it is presented (the big Other) that is decisive for its truthfulness.

Unconscious scenarios: the logic of fantasy

Since memory is not a perfect machine of representation of facts or original events (see Chapter 1, §1.2), Freud compares it in a later text to a children's toy called the mystic writing pad ('A Note upon the "Mystic Writing Pad" ', 1925). This toy consists of a thin sheet of plastic that covers a thick waxen board on which one can write with a pointed instrument. In the wax then appears a dark trace that can be removed by lifting the sheet. For Freud, this shows the psyche's recording of material (as a form of 'writing'). Memory covers a continuous rewriting of events; it is transcriptive.

To emphasize the importance of signifying elements in fantasy, Lacan recalls one of the first examples of Freud's analysis of fetishism (in 'Fetishism', 1927), on a man who spent his childhood in England. Later on in his life, when the man lived in Germany, he always sought 'ein Glanz auf der nase' that he subsequently tried to peep on. The German expression transposes the English expression 'a glance at the nose' that kept coming to mind since his early years (Lacan 1994: 158). Lacan stresses the *linguistic dimension* (signifiers) in the analysis of the fetish: the homophony of 'glance' and 'Glanz' that leads the man glancing at a 'Glanz', a shine or gleam, at the nose. Furthermore, signifiers that mark the limit of his recollection (for it is this phrase that he can recollect from his first years) mould his fantasmatic scene.

Lacan uses the phenomenon of fetishism to show a crucial aspect in the understanding of fantasy. Fantasy is not merely a question of the drives and their supposedly given 'innate images', but those 'innate images' are governed by a signifying function (a 'scheme') that determines the composition of the 'illusory object'. Thus we can reach further into the understanding of why, for instance, a female's shoe can provoke in a man the emergence of sexual energy that would seem to be destined for the reproduction of the species (Lacan 1998a: 229). The shoe, here, is not an innate object of the man's drives, but invested as a libidinal object because of its signifying function.

We must consider three dimensions in fantasy. There is the enjoyment that dominates, the images that cover up, and the signifiers that work (Ribettes 1984; Nasio 1987: 147). Lacan's second paradigm considers fantasy as more than the 'internal images' to which the drives are attached. From his fifth seminar onward, Lacan understands fantasy also as a *scenario* (cf. Miller 1999a: 11). When fantasy is a scenario, the image is subjected to the play of the signifier. We should remind ourselves here of Lacan's important statement on play.

> Only the subject – the human subject of the desire that is the essence of man – is not, unlike the animal, entirely caught up in this imaginary capture. He maps himself in it. How? In so far as he isolates the function of the screen and plays with it. Man, in effect, knows how to play with the mask.
>
> (Lacan 1998b: 107)[15]

It is the unconscious subject – of the signifier – that determines the formation of the fantasy. From the 'object' that my nostalgic desire longs for, only bits and pieces remain, which form the 'material' for fantasy to reconstruct the object (sounds, images, sayings). Those signifying elements are the 'material' of the unconscious; they belong to the domain of the Other. We shape the object of our desire by means of signifiers that we do not consciously choose. Thus we unconsciously 'write' a scenario, screenplay or script for the personage (character, role) we are in the 'other scene'.

Where Freud thought fantasies were related to childhood experiences by means of word-connections, Lacan interprets this relationship in terms of the signifier, the acoustic images of Saussure, which are detached from the concept (Verhaeghe 1999; Nobus 2000). The 'logic of fantasy' that Freud emphasizes is like that of an author when making a script, different wishes and beliefs often providing in the imagination protection and gratification simultaneously (Edelson 1988: 189). Where Freud discovered the laws of the primary process (condensation, displacement, inversion, etc.), Lacan poses the laws of the symbolic (grammar, syntax, combination, substitution). It shows that transformation is proper to fantasy (Perron-Borelli 2001: 124). For Lacan, there is a transformational grammar that directs the elementary structure of the unconscious (cf. Ribettes 1984: 190). Of these, the (dual) transformations of turning the active position into the passive (and inversely) is the most important ('turning against oneself', 'turning into the opposite'); the drive attains its goal via a modification of its activity.[16] Other important mechanisms of transformation consist of projection: I project onto the other what is coming from me ('she is in love with me instead of I'm in love with her'). And substitution: one object or activity is substituted for another.

The scheme of desire

Freud's crucial text on fantasy, 'A Child is Being Beaten', illustrates the 'signification (schematization) of pure desire' in Lacan's work. In this text,

Freud analyses the transformations – or avatars (Lacan 1998a: 237) – of a fantasy he regularly encounters in his therapeutic work, which comes down to the expression: 'A child is being beaten'. His patients use this fantasy in its conscious form (that is for Freud its 'third avatar') to generate libidinal pleasure: it often ends in acts of auto-erotic satisfaction. Freud discovers yet two previous forms of this (perverse) fantasy. The first form of this fantasy of chastisement, that probably once was conscious, comes down to the sentence: 'The father beats a child'. It expresses, according to Freud, the child's desire to be loved by the father – for the father beats the other child, hence does not love her. The second form of the fantasy is according to Freud so guilt-ridden that his patients cannot consciously remember it. Therefore, analysis must reconstruct it, and then the fantasy reads: 'I'm being beaten by the father'. It expresses for Freud an incestuous desire for the father, that the extreme feelings of guilt completely reverse, as a form of punishment, into its opposite (loving turns into hating/beating). The child, or the adult it becomes, uses the fantasy in the third form in such a way that its central figures are no longer identifiable. The fantasy apparently does not revolve at all around the child and its father, or around figures that are directly associated with them (siblings, teachers, etc). Therefore: '*a* child is being beaten'.

Lacan's analysis of this text considers the third form of this fantasy as nothing more than a *general scheme* (Lacan 1998a: 238). This final form of the fantasy gives – by means of signifiers – a specific (manageable, 'coherent', subjectivized, schematic) memorization or fixation of an impossible desire; something which retains for the subject the faculty to *constitute the privileged image* in which its genital satisfactions find support (Lacan 1998a: 239). So signifiers mould the images that both cover up and provide the enjoyment that dominates the fantasy-scene. This fantasy-subject of chastisement finds satisfaction in 'scenarios' in which 'someone is being beaten'. The repetition (replay, repeated performance) of some sort of 'beating' functions as a scheme, which provides the fantasy-subject the coordinates for 'drawing' the (empirical) object that can satisfy its desire.[17]

Fantasy *puts in* desire certain fixed 'traits', which, for instance, explain why someone continuously falls in love with the same person, or encounters the same kind of trouble in dealing with a certain issue. Like the Kantian subject of knowledge needs the scheme and the imagination as conditions for knowing an object the desiring subject only desires an object when it shows a 'scheme' (a 'trait', determined by signifiers) put in by the subject itself. The 'object' only appears to be desirable when it fits within the subject's fantasmatic (signifying) scheme. It resembles Kant's remark on mediation: 'This mediating representation must be pure (without anything empirical) and yet intellectual on the one hand and sensible on the other. Such a representation is the transcendental schema' (Kant 1789/1996: A 138). Fantasy, as a general scenario or scheme, allows desire – which is nothing but the formal structure of the subject – to find an object in the order of sensibility.

Defining signifiers

Lacan's reading of Freud's analysis of the man who always sought 'ein Glanz auf der nase' shows how in perversion the course of history is reduced to an instantaneous state (Lacan 1994: 119). In this case, fantasy projects, or freezes, desire into a fixed scenario. In psychoanalysis as a 'talking cure', such an objectification of desire must be extracted by uncovering the defining signifiers of the fantasy. What is at stake in psychoanalysis is to lay bare (reveal, bring to light) the determining unconscious signifiers (the 'unconscious Self'). Here are two examples.

Eric Laurent gives the example of a child being named a 'bad boy' by his mother. This child is

> represented as a 'bad boy' in relation to his mother's ideal. Thus 'bad boy' (or any other identification that served at one time as a master signifier) serves the subject as a guideline his whole life long. He is identified as such and behaves as such. At the very moment at which the subject identifies with such a signifier, he is petrified . . . Whenever you isolate one of the subject's identifications, what you then need to do is find the fantasy ($ ◊ *a*) that goes with it, the fantasy that brings him some jouissance.
>
> (Laurent 1995: 25)

In her text on 'The Drive', Marie-Hélène Brousse analyses how the signifier of the Other's demand defines the subject of the unconscious. She gives the following clinical example.

> I have a patient who is grappling with her mother's desire because she can't decide whether or not to have a baby. In reference to her mother's desire she can only remember one sentence. It's a memory of her mother being furious with her children, running after them and saying, 'I'm going to kill you'. The signifier of her mother's desire is 'I'm going to kill you'. In a sense, my patient was constituted on the basis of those signifiers, to kill a child. It's her interpretation of the Other's demand. The Other's demand is 'die!'
>
> (Brousse 1995: 109–110)

This example shows that the interpretation of what a significant other wants becomes the fantasy – a fantasy which, in the case of the aforementioned patients, should be 'untied' or 'worked through' to refloat their desire.

Fantasy gravitates around a defining signifier. Central to its scenario is the repetition of the 'unary trait', a signifier that is outside the chain of signifiers and which thus makes all signification possible – like the signifier 'die' determined for the mother all other meaning in regards to her desire to have a child. 'This latter signifier is therefore the signifier to which all the other signifiers represent the subject – which means that if this signifier is missing, all the other signifiers represent nothing' (Lacan 2006: 694). This signifier is 'undivided', as it is not related or made relative due to its relation to other signifiers, and Lacan therefore names it the One. It is the 'representative of all other representation'; 'representation's representative in the absolute condition is in its proper place in the unconscious, where it causes desire in accordance with the structure of fantasy' (Lacan 2006: 689).[18]

The signifiers that determine the fundamental fantasy are not – like all the other signifiers – relative, but have an absolute signification (like the signifier 'die' in the aforementioned example). 'They are not transcendent signifiers; they are indices of an absolute signification, a notion which will, I hope, seem appropriate to the condition of fantasy' (Lacan 2006: 691). Those determining signifiers are 'absolute', outside ('absolved from') the ordinary chains of signification (i.e. they are nonsensical): 'Interpretation is directed not so much at meaning as at reducing signifiers to their non-meaning so as to find the determinants of the whole of the subject's behavior' (Lacan, in Laurent 1995: 26).

The formula of fantasy: Lacan beyond Klein

The unconscious is where there is an 'insignificant' gap in the (conscious) discourse of the subject. Lacan expresses this in the form of a lozenge [◊].

> I have been able to articulate the unconscious for you as being situated in the gaps that the distribution of the signifying investments sets up in the subject, and which figure in the algorithm in the form of a losange [◊], which I place at the centre of any relation of the unconscious between reality and the subject.
>
> (Lacan 1998b: 181)

The unconscious must be situated in the gap, as a linguistic phenomenon: the unconscious is structured as a language. It is by means of language, and its transformational grammar, that the subject of desire 'fills in' this gap. The result is that the object of desire is polymorphous.[19]

With a reference to Freud's notion of the 'overdetermination' of symptoms – they never have simply one cause but are a 'composition' – Lacan brings forward his fundamental idea of language 'multiplying' the object of man's needs and demands. As it detaches us from the immediacy of the need, language (the order of signifiers) opens up the space of multiple scenes that shape the object. The *object* of desire thus disappears into a multiplicity of *scenes*.

> It [the overdetermination of symptoms] means that interference will occur in the effects that correspond in a subject to a particular demand from the effects of a position that he maintains as a subject in relation to the other (here, his semblable). 'That he maintains as subject' means that language allows him to regard himself as the stagehand, or even the director, of the entire imaginary capture of which he would otherwise be nothing more than the living marionette. Fantasy is the very illustration of this original possibility. That is why any temptation to reduce fantasy to imagination, that doesn't admit to its failure, is a permanent misconception, a misconception from which the Kleinian school, which has certainly carried things very far here, is not free, having failed to even glimpse the category of the signifier. However, the notion of the unconscious fantasy no longer presents any difficulty once it is defined as an image set to work in the signifying structure.
>
> (Lacan 2006: 532)

Bringing Lacan's theory of fantasy into the 'Controversial Discussions' mentioned earlier (see Chapter 2, §2.3) might help to summarize its position. Lacan refines the 'Kleinian' opposition between conscious *f*antasies and unconscious *ph*antasies, from his own (early) theoretical framework. It is impossible, he says in 1958, to usefully distinguish the unconscious fantasies from the play of imagination if we do not see that the signifier structures the unconscious fantasy (Lacan 1998a: 252–253). Fantasies are unconscious because signifiers from the realm of the Other, and their laws, structure them outside our conscious awareness: the fantasy-image is 'set to work in a signifying structure'. That differentiates them from conscious constructions by the ego for gaining pleasure (although also this play of imagination may be the more acceptable version of unconscious fantasies).

For Lacan, one cannot speak of a 'true reality' of the content of primary mental processes: there are no original and primitive objects that correspond 'naturally' to our 'deepest wishes'. Lacan disagrees with the Kleinian idea of 'phantasy' that supposes an intuitive recognition by the drive of its object. 'The objects are already, if I may express me that way, *signifiered* (*signifiantisés*)' (Lacan 1998a: 253; my translation). The substitution of reality by means of the signifier is original.

Lacan expresses this steering aspect of the signifier in the formula of fantasy that he uses from 1957 onward: $\$ \lozenge a$. Fantasy consists of heterogeneous elements; it connects the *libinal* (the object of enjoyment) to the *symbolical* (the subject of the signifier). Thus there is a virtualization of *jouissance* (the excessive enjoyment beyond the pleasure principle that is delightful and painful at the same time).[20] For human beings, *jouissance* is mostly not a brute act of consumption but organized by and within the limits of the symbolical order (which is expressed in the crucial term 'surplus-enjoyment'; see

Chapter 6, §6.3). So Lacan's formula of fantasy expresses that signifying elements bring the enjoyment of the fantasy-object (*a*) on a symbolical level: it makes one think of 'enjoyment in the signifier'. Fantasy brings the real of *jouissance* that the drives seek at the level of representation; it covers both the *subject of language* and the *subject of the body* (Verhaeghe 2001). It interfaces both domains.

4

DEFENCE

Fantasy as a screen

4.1 Traumatism

'Medusa's Head'

> I cannot help remembering a remark of De Casseres. It was over the wine in Mouquin's. Said he: 'The profoundest instinct in man is to war against the truth; that is, against the Real. He shuns facts from his infancy. His life is a perpetual evasion. Miracle, chimera and tomorrow keep him alive. He lives on fiction and myth. It is the Lie that makes him free. Animals alone are given the privilege of lifting the veil of Isis; men dare not. The animal, awake, has no fictional escape from the Real because he has no imagination. Man, awake, is compelled to seek a perpetual escape into Hope, Belief, Fable, Art, God, Socialism, Immortality, Alcohol, Love. From Medusa-Truth he makes an appeal to Maya-Lie.
>
> (Jack London, *The Mutiny of the Elsinore*)

In Greek mythology, Medusa is a Gorgon monster with hair consisting of serpents and a face so terrible that directly looking upon her would turn the onlooker into stone. She was beheaded by the hero Perseus who used her head as a weapon. To perform this act of killing, he had to look at her harmless reflection in the mirror instead of directly at her, to prevent him from also being turned into stone.

In his 1922 article 'Medusa's Head', which was only published posthumously in 1940, Freud elaborates the phenomenon of the 'gaze of Medusa', which, according to him, functions as the source (the real) of castration. Medusa is presented as 'the supreme talisman who provides the image of castration – associated in the child's mind with the discovery of maternal sexuality – and its denial' (Freud 1940: 273). In psychoanalytic theory, the myth of Medusa is the representation of the confrontation with the 'lack', and the ways in which humans use images to deny this horrific truth. For Lacan, the meeting with the head of Medusa signifies a direct confrontation with the real: a confrontation that 'freezes' the subject.

> this real Medusa's head, the revelation of this something which properly speaking is unnameable . . . there's an anxiety-provoking revelation of an image which summarizes what we can call the revelation of that which is least penetrable in the real, of the real lacking any possible mediation, of the ultimate real.
>
> (Lacan 1988b: 164)

The myth of Medusa shows that individuals use protective images to defend themselves against petrifaction by the other's look. In neurosis, for instance, the other's look is often experienced with an 'uncanny' feeling, and the neurotic tries to defend himself against this by hiding in his self-created world of fantasy-images. In psychosis, the look can be experienced so intensively that it amounts to a feeling of persecution: the psychotic is constantly under a (direct) control of the look of the other, without the (protective) mediation of regular consciousness. And in perversion the look, focused on sex, plays an important role in the genealogy of perversions: the pervert is the one who is playing with images to both manifest and deny the castrating awareness of the lack.

For Lacan, the real is the order of things that is beyond our ability and capability to perceive directly, and for that reason it is traumatic. It cannot be integrated in an unmediated manner into our (imaginary and symbolic) reality.[1] The real, Lacan says, is the impossible, and fantasy is a 'screen' that mediates our relation to this 'hidden' aspect of our reality. Take for instance Freud's case study of the Wolf Man (see next section). 'The exceptional importance of this case in Freud's work is to show that it is in relation to the real that the level of fantasy functions. The real supports the fantasy, the fantasy protects the real' (Lacan 1998b: 41). As such, fantasy has a protective function. It is a *defence* against a traumatic awareness. Thus fantasy *supports* desire by staging its objects. Anxiety is the too close approximation of the non-representable object: the impossible object of desire is not sufficiently kept at a distance by the fantasy-screen.[2] Lacan's theory of fantasy as a screen centres on the idea that, to put it elliptical, behind the screen there is something that is not. Behind the reality sustained by the screen there is not a transcendent, given 'true' reality. Actually, behind the screen there is a void, a non-representable real.

To illuminate this, I will now elaborate Lacan's notion of the real. In Section 4.2, I will then return to the point that fantasy is a defensive screen set up against this traumatic real.

More real than reality

Freud teaches us that trauma is what cannot be remembered and against which the subject sets up defensive organizations in his psyche. It resists direct recollection and articulation (and thus interpretation). In the fifth chapter of *The Four Fundamental Concepts of Psychoanalysis*, Lacan explains his theory of the *real as trauma*. In this context, Lacan discusses a dream described by Freud in chapter seven of *The Interpretation of Dreams*. There Freud recounts a father who lost his son and went to sleep in the room beside the one in which his dead son lay, leaving an old man to watch over his son. After several hours of sleep, the father dreams that the child is near his bed, taking him by the arm and whispering reproachfully: 'Father, can't you see that I am burning?' The father wakes up and notices a bright light coming from the other room. He rushes into the room and finds the old man asleep and the clothes and one arm of the child scorched by a candle that fell onto the corpse.

According to Freud, this dream is motivated (partially) by the fulfilment of wishes: the father wants to see his child alive once more and therefore is not awakened by the light until after the scene with his son. Although Freud admits that the interpretation of the dream is not complete, it does not deviate from his theory of dreams as wish-fulfilments. Lacan considers this example as a not very steady confirmation of the thesis of dreams as realizations of desire. He sees another function emerging in this dream. The father does not so much awaken because of the light, after having realized his desire to see his son once more, but he awakes because he is confronted *in the dream* with *another reality* that carries more weight than he can bear. Lacan suggests that the words the child addresses to his father – the significance of which Freud is not conclusive about – express the cause of the child's death.

In his analysis of this dream, Lacan hence focuses on something that is more real than the dream's psychical reality. Where in the common understanding of psychoanalysis the psychical reality of dreams is supposed to express our desires and deepest truth, Lacan, surprisingly, states that the level of representations in a dream is not the final dimension of desire. For that is what those representations hide: 'The real has to be sought beyond the dream – in what the dream has enveloped, hidden from us' (Lacan 1998b: 60). So where Freud finds something that he calls the 'navel of the dream', Lacan discovers the relation to a non-interpretable real.

In his famous case of the Wolf Man, Freud leads the obsessional neurosis of his patient back to the centrality of his patient's dream about wolves. In that dream, wolves suddenly appear in the patient's bedroom window. According to Freud – via a long interpretation – this refers to the primal scene in which the child sees its parents copulating. For Lacan, those representatives (the wolves) function as a representative of the subject's encounter with the real (of traumatic *jouissance*) – not necessarily of the subject's encounter with the primal scene. So where Freud speaks of an unconscious fixation to a repressed desire, Lacanian theory focuses more on the representatives of such 'unconscious desire'.[3] Such representatives are pivotal in the psychic life of the Wolf Man, although not 'analogue' to or deducible from 'real reality'. They are composited from different elements in order *to represent*, and at the same time *to cover up*, the (traumatic) *jouissance*. As such, those representatives construct the formal frame of our desire, our fundamental fantasy.[4]

The impossible

The notion of the real is crucial for what is the central concern of psychoanalysis, namely the status of the object of the drives and hence of desire. As a desiring being, man wants to undo the loss that is constitutive of his existence, which means that at the level of the drives he wants to regain gratification. In a general sense, the real relates very closely to what Freudo-Lacanian theory calls 'the lost object', the object of 'lost', 'prohibited' or 'impossible' gratifications. As a general theory on the constitution of subjectivity, it surpasses the psychopathological field of the trauma and reaches far into the field of (philosophical) anthropology. As such, it does not concern itself primarily, to use the words of Lacan's student Serge Leclaire, with the traumatic event but with the *traumatism* (or the violence or excess) that the 'lost object' itself causes (Leclaire 1971: 26–27).[5] The trauma and the defences (whose interaction bring us close to the notion of fantasy) make up not just the pathological individual. Everybody must take a stance with regards to the lack that inevitably hits us as a human being, death being obviously the crudest intruder on our daily existence.

With reason Lacan opposes Plato's myth about an existence that the Other can supplement. He replaces it through his myth of the lamella wherein human existence inevitably goes along with a real loss, namely death. Instead of (Platonic) reminiscence, the phenomenon of repetition becomes a central issue, for the real is the *cause of repetition*. Due to the fact that the real is non-representational there is repetition, making the subject return to the place of the lost object, the lost satisfaction. Compared with the lost satisfaction every other satisfaction pales. The subject repetitively returns to the site of that absence in the hope of finding the *real Thing*, and yet forever missing it (Fink 1995: 228). Repetition may even characterize life itself: man keeps on reproducing himself, he keeps on elaborating the same old questions because an answer is lacking, etc. We might say that we even keep on having sex over and over again because we cannot truly reach the other at the level of speech: 'Encore' (which indicates the failure of Platonic love). Because of the failure to say what we want to say, we reproduce ourselves (Lacan 1999: 109). That is what Lacan is talking about when he says that the sexual relation does not exist. If the sexual relation did exist, Lacan says, we could touch the other at the level of the signifier. But as speaking beings we are solitary. There is no signifier that can present and represent the opposite sex in a pure state – or it must be at the cellular level: one calls that the sexual chromosome (Lacan 1966–1967: 19 April 1967). Fantasy is the result of this impossibility.

A general characteristic of the real is its function as a limit: *the real is the impossible* (Lacan 1991: 143):

> since the opposite of the possible is certainly the real, we would be lead to define the real as the impossible.
>
> (Lacan 1998b: 167)

The real is an impossible presence: impossible to sustain (as in anxiety) or to confront (thus leading, for instance, to phobia); impossible to achieve in space or time; impossible to represent or symbolize. With the category of the real Lacan thinks an ontological category that is beyond the constitutive activities of the subject. Not everything that we say or do is the result of our unconscious desire (see the dream of the burning son). There is no core of 'full signification' at the heart of our desire. Desire is, in contrast, the result of the distance from the real. This notion of the real underwrites that life is not a dream and psychoanalysis not an idealism (cf. Lacan 1998b: 53). The return of the real (in slips, symptoms, disruptions) warrants this truth.

To cover the notion of the real that plays such an important role in Lacan's (later) work, and that nevertheless is so hard to grasp, we will take a look at how his work developed it.

Three paradigms of the real

In her overview of the real, Ellie Ragland refers to Jacques-Alain Miller's periodization of Lacan's teachings to cover Lacan's elaboration of the real. In the 1950s, Lacan describes the real as concrete and already full, a brute, *pre-symbolic reality* that returns to the same place (Ragland 1996: 192). Lacan points out that the stars manifested first and foremost the notion of a being that is 'always in the same place' (Lacan 1988b: 238). He illuminates the dialectic between the real and the symbolic when he advances that it is not fully explicable why human beings saw the Big Bear or Orion in a certain constellation of stars. He uses this example to found his theory of the arbitrariness of the symbol, as man's symbolical representation of a group of stars is not fully deductible from its 'inherent form'. Symbolic systems *structure* the real rather than *reflecting* the real, as images pretend to do with their mimetic forms of representation. 'The famous properties of form do not seem to provide an absolutely convincing explanation of the way in which we have grouped the constellations' (Lacan 1988b: 238). In the 1950s, Lacan considers the real as a sort of function of constancy that we must necessarily assume to be lying behind the symbolic formations that are his primary concern (alienation is the pivotal term). In this period, structuralism reigned supreme and steered his teaching to a theorization of the subject in which the human psyche almost dissolves into a superstructure of symbols with almost no bond to the physical body. In this approach, the real is hence less important for the understanding of human reality, which is determined by the big Other of language. But the notion of the real becomes increasingly important in his theory.

In the second period of his teaching, the 1960s and early 1970s, Lacan links the real to the Freudian Thing (Ragland 1996: 195), and hence to *trauma*. According to Freud, 'das Ding' is the aspect of the fellow human being or neighbour that we cannot grasp or understand. Lacan translates 'das Ding' as the object in the Other, which cannot be signified by the signifying chain, although this chain necessarily circles around it. So there are some similarities with his previous notion of the real as a necessary function of materiality 'underneath' the symbolic order. Yet the impact of the real is now much bigger, as the subject comes into being *as a defence against it*, against the primal experience of pleasure/pain associated with it (Fink 1999: 95). The real becomes the central element in Lacan's theory of the trauma. This traumatic element can hit us from two directions. From outside of ourselves, as in the case – albeit in a weak form – of a reprimand that 'awakes' us from our self-satisfied world.[6] Or from within, such as deep feelings of affection that paralyse us. The Thing is 'what hurts', the external traumatic *X* derailing the Self of the pleasure principle that circles around hallucinatory objects (Freud's *Lust-Ich*), and forcing it to 'confront reality'; yet the Thing is simultaneously the subject's innermost kernel of his being, what he must sacrifice to gain access to external reality (Žižek 1993: 90). The Other (inside or outside ourselves) is not just a symbolic presence but manifests itself as a (traumatic) *encounter*. That is the real aspect of the Other, which Lacan attributes to his former purely symbolic Other. The Other is also a 'real Thing' – imagined in horror movies as a monster or as the alien inside ourselves. As 'the Thing' discloses an aspect of reality that is hardly bearable for the Self of the pleasure principle, the subject tries to defend itself against its overwhelming impact by integrating the traumatic *jouissance* into the limits of the pleasure principle. The pleasure principle is the principle that seeks to regulate excitation (a regulation comparable to making a good horror movie on the destructive force of death, a sort of movie that in Lacanian terms plays with the thin line between pleasure and *jouissance*). This mediation of *jouissance* is pivotal for understanding the defensive aspect of fantasy.

From the early 1970s until his death in 1981, Lacan aligns his elaboration of the real with Freud's attempts from the 1920s onward to explain the difference between the sexes, and hence he focuses on the *real as jouissance* of the body. Lacan seeks to advance psychoanalysis where Freud found a dead-end, where the non-rapport between the sexes – the asymmetry or fundamental differences that constitute the masculine in culture or the feminine in culture – is a reality (Ragland 1996: 199). The impossibility that the real stands for now seems to be pulled out of the theory of the individual trauma and repositioned in the cultural field as the subject's radical impossibility, through its singular *jouissance*, its mode of enjoying, of reaching the Other. An impossibility that Lacan indicates with his infamous phrase that 'there is no sexual relationship'. In that they are situated differently with regards to the law and have a different kind of *jouissance*, man and woman will never supplement each other. Although this is one of the most difficult chapters in the Lacanian discourse, it seems to be Lacan's focus on the *jouissance* of the body (the body as a libidinal organism that enjoys) that establishes the general view on the radical impossibility of clear communication. The result is that the 'real' of the symptom, the truth it refers to, is not situated so much anymore at the level of its (true) meaning or at the level of original events from which it might arise, but at the level of bodily *jouissance* as a satisfaction of drives. Lacan ends up with a theory that returns to the Freudian libido-theory, wherein the desiring subject gravitates around drive-fixations (cf. Thurston 2002; see also Chapter 5, §5.2). This would be Lacan's final 'return to Freud'.

4.2 Screen

> For desire is a defense, a defense against going beyond a limit in jouissance.
>
> (Lacan 2006: 699)

Anxiety

> It is obvious that the inventory of the imaginary, from the great sacred myths to the purely aesthetic emotions, is completely oriented by its fundamental inspiration: to escape death and the vicissitudes of time . . . The struggle against decay, the exorcism of death and temporal decomposition: such is, in our view, the euphemising function of the imagination as a whole.
>
> (Durand 1999: 391)

This is what Gilbert Durand concludes in his grand work on the role of the imaginary in human existence. The imaginary is a distanciation from a real that is anxiety-provoking.

To understand the function of fantasy, it is crucial to have a grasp of the fundamental phenomenon in psychoanalysis: anxiety. For Lacan, anxiety is an affection, and not an emotion. Furthermore, it is the only affection that is not deceptive (cf. Lacan 1998b: 41). That is, it is an affection with a *real* object. The real as the *object of anxiety* implies that nothing is as bad as not missing the 'real Thing', that is to say getting it. In his theory of anxiety, especially as put forward in his 1962–1963 seminar of the same name, Lacan engages in a polemic with other theories by stating that anxiety *does* have an object. Paradoxically, this object of anxiety is the lost object of desire. So anxiety occurs when we are not enough at a distance – 'separated' – from the object of ultimate enjoyment that simultaneously annihilates us as a singularized subject (where pleasure topples into *jouissance*). It is not the absence of the object of desire that causes anxiety, but its proximity! It is on this point that Lacan differs from Freud. For where Freud holds that one of the causes of anxiety is separation from the mother, Lacan considers precisely a lack of such separation to induce anxiety.

The anxiety Lacan analyses seems to be a 'psychotic anxiety', an experience of losing oneself, which can occur when nothing is lacking anymore: anxiety is the lack of lacking. Someone who endlessly tries to think out who he is, or who tries to objectify himself completely (for instance, by ceaselessly staring into the mirror) may get to a point where he no longer knows who he is. Trying to get to the 'real thing' in the mirror image may crush the identification with the image that provides and regulates our usual self-awareness (some sort of veiling is necessary). Furthermore, there is the well-known idea that it might be more horrifying to obtain the 'real Thing' of eternal life than not to have it (fictionally exemplified by the undead existence of zombies). Anxiety indicates that the distance to the real (the emptiness, negativity or lack that causes desire) is about to disappear, and the screen of fantasy is at the point of collapsing. An intimate or intense approaching of the real annihilates the lack; it cancels out the distance (between representation and the object as it is 'in itself'); it cancels out the difference that causes desire and makes the space for fantasy. At a superficial level, this implies that when one obtains an object that one desires, it is hardly ever as good as one thought it to be (for then it was supplemented, or even supported by our fantasy about it). At a more profound level, it means that the realization of a dream can turn out to be a nightmare.

The veil

It is the non-mediation of the real that causes anxiety. As long as we desire – that is, supplement the real with our fantasy and thus support our reality – we keep anxiety at a distance. 'Desire is certainly intolerable but it protects the subject against the human tendency in all of us that seeks the extreme limit' (Nasio 1998: 90). As Lacan argues in his 1960–1961 seminar on transference, desire is a remedy for anxiety. Also love, as a form of desire, is a remedy for anxiety, by giving an imaginary-symbolic form to the object of desire that one can never fully assimilate. For what we love in the other, Lacan says, is something that lies beyond the qualities of the other (a mysterious *X* that causes our desire). We can only speak imaginatively about what it is that we love in the other, without actually grasping it.[7]

Lacan exemplifies this theory of the screen by referring to perceptual experiments in which one can only see an object whose rays of light blind us, through a screen that mitigates their impact.

> I alluded to the reference given by Maurice Merleau-Ponty in *La phénoménologie de la perception* in which, from well-chosen examples

based on the experiments of Gelb and Goldstein, one can already see, simply at the perceptual level, how the screen re-establishes things, in their status as real. If, by being isolated, an effect of lighting dominates us, if, for example, a beam of light directing our gaze so captivates us that it appears as a milky cone and prevents us from seeing what it illuminates, the mere fact of introducing into this field a small screen, which cuts into that what is illuminated without being seen, makes the milky light retreat, as it were, into the shadow, and allows the object it concealed to emerge. At the perceptual level, this is the phenomenon of a relation that is to be taken in a more essential function, namely, that in its relation to desire, reality appears only as marginal.

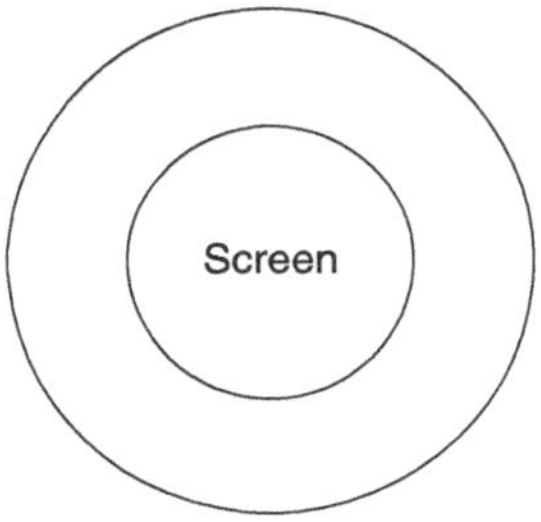

reality is marginal

(Lacan 1998b: 107–108)

The 'madness' of amorousness may illuminate this. One does not dare to look the person that causes the amorous feelings straight in the face, and one's regard hence dwells with all the persons that surround her/him, who are not so emotionally charged. This 'neutral surrounding' is then indeed marginal compared with the 'object' that causes desire. The screen of fantasy is a necessary formation of the object and hence a mediation of the psychical intensity associated with the real. Lacan develops this notion of the object-cause of desire as the *object a*. In his exposition on 'The Function of the Veil' in his 1956–1957 seminar on the object-relation, he still thinks this 'object' as an absence that we can present only symbolically, by means of signifiers. We need signifiers in order to deal with it and to construct it. And this is what love does; it generates also a symbolical relation to what one cannot grasp. Thus it differs from amorousness, in which we love the image of the other, and which is therefore a predominantly imaginary phenomenon (see Roland Barthes' *A Lover's Discourse* for the articulation and imagination of love and amorousness).

Since our ego is an inevitable mediator of self and other (see Chapter 2, §2.2), also love cannot avoid having a narcissistic structure (cf. Lacan 1998b:

186). This imagining is necessary to install a relation to this beyond: no symbolical relation (with absence) without the imaginary (Lacan 1994: 57). All of man's symbols testify to this.[8] This aspect of symbolic and imaginary mediation shows how fantasmatic desire is a (necessary) medium: the fantasmatic relation to the object is the libidinal motivation of our odyssey through the world.

Phenomena like love bring us to Lacan's scheme of the veil (Lacan 1994: 156):

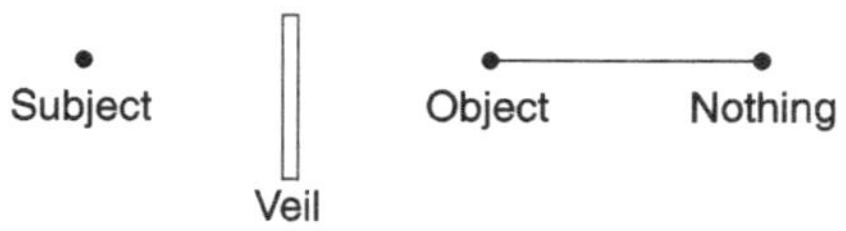

The veil is that on which the absence can 'paint' itself, where the subject can project and imagine the 'impossible' object of desire (the traumatic or mysterious *X*, the object-cause of desire). On the veil, the imagined object can take the place of the lack. Lacan uses one of the most fundamental images of man's mediation, the 'veil of Maya', to express this relation of interposition. This veil is a powerful metaphor to express the relationship of man to everything that captivates him, for there is 'a certain fundamental illusion in all the relations that are interweaved with his desire' (Lacan 1994: 155; my translation).

We compose reality around the fundamental fantasmatic relation to the real object of desire (i.e. we are moved by our fundamental fantasies). That what one cannot name (in love, in art) motivates the efforts to appropriate this 'object' and leads to its phenomenal construction. Lacan expresses this pivotal notion in a number of ways. He speaks of the real as a hole in reality that fantasy fills. Also his description of the real object (*a*) of desire as the semblant of being expresses this notion of the fantasy-screen that mediates the real; the fantasmatic object supports being (Lacan 1999: 87). As an ontology his theory brings forward that we only know the appearances of being. At the psychical level, reality takes shape at the surface. It gravitates around our fantasmatic relation to an inaccessible real. Fantasy is therefore what sustains the position of the symbolic subject.

Pleasure and the mediation of jouissance

Freudian psychoanalysis considers man to be an excessive animal that tries to regain, hazard, and maintain his (mental) balance in relation to what Lacan calls the (traumatic) real of *jouissance*. A commonly made mistake is to confuse this enjoyment with feelings of pleasure. But if one wants to have an idea of what Lacan means by enjoyment, the first thing to do is to let go of this confusion. Enjoyment is not pleasure! It can be found exactly there where the regulation of the psyche by means of the principles of pleasure and displeasure reaches its limits; where the subject touches upon its limits, the real.

The excitement that seizes someone who drives his car as fast as possible is not pleasure. The excitement of a voyeur who can be caught at any moment in his act of looking is not simply pleasure. *Jouissance* is a state beyond pleasure; or in Freud's terms, it is an excessive tension, a maximum tension, whereas pleasure is a diminution of tension! (Nasio 1998: 106). Pleasure is a category that belongs to the imaginary domain; it 'works' with images. Pleasure always depends on the coming and going of images and is thus a sensation perceived and experienced by the (thinking) ego. However, 'Lacan, inspired by the cogito of Descartes, located the position of the subject in the state of *jouissance* by stating "I am there where I do not think"' (Nasio 1998: 39–40). Enjoying is even dissimilar from feeling, if one comprehends feeling as a conscious process, as a conscious noticing of sensations.

Fantasy functions as a screen with regards to an enjoyment that is too excessive, traumatic. As such, it reduces ('writes down', 'traces') *jouissance* within the rules and principles of the imaginary and of the law (the imaginary and symbolic order). It has the fundamental tendency to limit too excessive forms of excitement and bring them within the homeostatic borders of the pleasure principle.

> The function of the pleasure principle is, in effect, to lead the subject from signifier to signifier, by generating as many signifiers as are required to maintain at as low a level as possible the tension that regulates the whole functioning of the psychic apparatus.
>
> (Lacan 1992: 119)

Actually, psychoanalysis advocates that fantasy has no other function than to temper this excessive *jouissance* (Ribettes 1984: 192). At the same time, fantasy preserves in this protective function something of the *jouissance* it tries to temper, by transforming it, imagining it. The example of 'online cheating' may illustrate this. Playing these 'imaginary' scenes may be a way to deal with and give form to one's 'wild' and 'unknown' sexual drives. In directing the drives, the scenes may prevent libidinal energies from freely fleeting and being destructive. And this 'formation' also gives a certain pleasure to the subject.

In *Beyond the Pleasure Principle*, Freud discerns two forms of the 'beyond of the pleasure principle'. The first *precedes* the pleasure principle. His analysis of repetition of painful dreams in traumatic neuroses and the repetition of the departure of the mother in a child's play shows that there are phenomena that seem to contradict the mechanism of the pleasure principle. For the pleasure principle is first of all a mechanism to *avoid displeasure*: the psychic apparatus aims at keeping the quantity of tension or excitement as low as possible, or at least at a constant level. Freud argues that the repetition of painful events functions as a capturing of energies that are not bound. It binds the energies of the trauma to certain representations.[9] As such, it is preliminary to the opposition of pleasure and displeasure. By binding the energies it actually installs the pleasure principle, for this is a principle that functions at the level of psychic representations. It controls the excitement that is associated with certain representations. Because of this binding of excitement to (imaginary) representations, the pleasure principle functions at the level of the Lacanian imaginary. The second 'beyond' that Freud discerns *exceeds* the pleasure principle. The death drive consists of the unbinding of the mediated representation of excitement, and is hence characterized by the loss of control over excitement. It disrupts the imaginary order of the pleasure principle.

In Freudo-Lacanian psychoanalysis, fantasy is related to the pleasure principle, the principle of homeostasis, in a double way. Fantasy makes its functioning possible by binding the excessive energies to representations. And after it has conditioned the pleasure principle, it organizes 'situations' wherein man can experience something of the lost *jouissance* (like watching a film). Fantasy both *closes* and *discloses*; it protects us from the real and opens up our reality at the same time.

5

MEDIATION

Where reality and fantasy converge

5.1 Fantasy and the law

Castration

The Oedipus complex is for the child the first major transition to the realm of social relations. It installs the intrapsychic principles for relating to others (the law). For Freud, there are unconscious desires and fantasies before the end of the Oedipus complex. From a Lacanian point of view, desire proper does not exist before the introduction of the law, the fundamental principles underlying all social relations. For Lacan, desire is the result of the 'prohibition' demanded by the 'Father' in the Oedipus complex. 'Castration means that jouissance has to be refused in order to be attained on the inverse scale of the Law of desire' (Lacan 2006: 700). For Lacan, castration is the term that implies for both the boy and the girl the exit from the Oedipus complex.[1]

The law manifests itself first of all as a prohibition of 'imaginary plenitude'. In the strict Freudian terminology – that I will not follow here – this implies for the child struggling in the triangular situation of the Oedipus complex (mother, father, and child) a prohibition of incest, of being the 'imaginary phallus' for the mother, the one who can fulfil her desire.

> But Freud reveals to us that it is thanks to the Name-of-the-Father that man does not remain bound to the sexual service of his mother, that aggression against the Father is at the very heart of the Law, and that the Law is in the service of desire that Law institutes through the prohibition of incest.
>
> (Lacan 1996: 418)

Castration is the symbolic act of imposing the lack (of renouncing 'imaginary plenitude').[2] As its result, a (symbolic) subject of desire emerges, which must retrace this *jouissance* within the limits of the law defining social reality.

> We must keep in mind that jouissance is prohibited [*interdite*] to whoever speaks, as such – or, put differently, it can only be said [*dite*] between the lines by whoever is subject of the Law, since the Law is founded on that very prohibition.
>
> (Lacan 2006: 696)

After castration, this 'lost enjoyment' is what we only can have a glance upon through the grid of language. We must try to *find it back* by *articulating* our desire. But because of this articulation, this enjoyment then is dispersed, fragmented, and partial.

The assumption of the castration has a normalizing effect (castration can also be denied). It is for the subject the condition for developing a desire of its own, and not getting stuck in an imaginary world of rivalry and aggressivity. 'Thus it is, rather, the assumption of castration that creates the lack on the basis of which desire is instituted' (Lacan 1996: 418). As the symbolic subject of desire tries to reorganize the lost object by means of fantasy (staging the object, 'making scenes'), it is fantasy that guides the reality of the subject after castration. So, from castration results 'that there is no cause of desire than produced by that operation, and that fantasy dominates all the reality of desire' (Lacan 1991: my translation)

As it is not possible to accept castration entirely, the subject of desire never fully achieves a completely 'normal' position. The way in which the subject deals with castration is decisive for the unconscious position that it takes. Lacan therefore begins his text 'The Signification of the Phallus' with the following finding:

> We know that the unconscious castration complex functions as a knot:
>
> 1 in the dynamic structuring of symptoms, in the analytic sense of the term, in other words, in the dynamic structuring of what is analyzable in the neuroses, perversions, and psychoses;
> 2 in regulating the development that gives its *ratio* to this first role: namely, the instating in the subject of an unconscious position without which he could not identify with the ideal type of his sex or even answer the needs of his partner in sexual relations without grave risk, much less appropriately meet the needs of the child who may be produced thereby.
>
> (Lacan 2006: 575)

The vicissitudes of our acceptation of 'the lack' determine our unconscious position, our identity, and our being in the world (it even touches upon our children's being). As this acceptance is never perfect (for that would make us disappear as a person in some sort of Nirvana), psychical reality always contains a fantasmatic element: there is no 'pure desire'. Therefore, all of us are to a certain extent wrapped up in the 'fundamental illusions' of one of the three subject-positions that Lacanian theory develops. I shall address briefly those three fundamental structures (cf. Verhaeghe 1994: 186–192).

Neurosis

> The ego has come into conflict with the id in the service of the super-ego and of reality; and this is the state of affairs in every transference neurosis.
>
> (Freud 1924: 150)

For Freud, neurosis is basically the result of an intrapsychic conflict in which the ego must defend itself against the instinctual demands of the id, as well as comply with the moral demands of the super-ego. The simulated neurosis of the transference relation between analysand and analyst works this conflict out.[3] For Freud, the distinction between neurosis and normality is only quantitaive, so that neurosis, in principle, can be cured. For Lacan, however, there is no such thing as 'normalcy' and neurosis is therefore one of the three inevitable structures of desire. The idea of eliminating the structure at all and attain normalcy is an illusion.

Neurosis is the structure in which the subject does recognize its limitations (the 'lack' imposed by the law: castration) but at the same time struggles to escape this situation. Neurotic symptoms are the signs of this struggle between unconscious desire and the demands of reality (they are 'compromise formations'). The (unconscious) fantasy that accompanies this structure is that of an imaginary wholeness (the 'paradise', a world without lack). The fact that this kind of fantasy is not played out (as in perversion) but remains *repressed* is exactly what makes the subject neurotic.

Lacan's notion of neurosis as one of the fundamental structures of human desire is less unfamiliar when understanding that he conceives of neurosis as the result of a question, namely the question that being raises for the subject: 'whether phobic, hysterical, or obsessive, neurosis is a question that being raises for the subject "from where he was before the subject came into the world" (this subordinate clause is the very expression Freud uses in explaining the Oedipus complex to little Hans). At stake here is the being that appears in a split second in the emptiness of the verb "to be" and, as I said, this being raises its question for the subject' (Lacan 2006: 432). Neurosis spins around the question of being and non-being, existence and death: 'why am I here?', 'what does it mean to be alive?' These questions concerning the contingency of existence may hit all of us, and as there is no final answer to them ('no solution in the signifier') it is hard to leave them out of consideration. Nevertheless, they may also lead to endless doubt, and make the desiring subject a pathological neurotic developing a set of symptoms – as in obsessional neurosis and hysteria.

Characteristic of neurosis in both its hysteric and obsessional form is the all-embracing sense of guilt. For the neurotic, the object that he (necessarily turns himself into) is never 'it': the characteristic doubt of the neurotic. The hysteric refuses to be in any possible way the object of others' enjoyment: 'I am not that'. The neurotic experiences all identifications as alienating, and he fantasizes of 'the real thing'. But as he always remains within the domain of the law, he will never get 'it'.

In hysteria, the guiding question concerns sexual identity and the relation between the sexes ('Am I a man or a woman?'). The hysteric continually doubts what her position in this field is, and it is this uncertainty that characterizes her desire.[4] Therefore, Lacan designates hysteria as the showing in action of the unconscious: because lack is so decisive for the hysteric's desire, there is a privileged relation between the structure of hysteria and that of desire. However, in hysteria desire becomes problematic, as everything is aimed at keeping desire unsatisfied. The hysteric refuses to be an object (of desire, of enjoyment) for the other. At the same time, her desire is completely directed at the other: the fundamental uncertainty concerning the hysteric's position makes her look for a master. However, whenever the other answers or approaches, the hysteric jumps away: desire must remain unsatisfied, open, at all costs. Also, the hysteric remains guided by an unconscious fantasy of an existence without castration, a law without limitation.

For an obsessional, the ultimate question concerns his own being: 'why am I here', 'who am I?' As the obsessional considers it unbearable that the question does not have a final answer, he defends himself from this impossibility by turning towards the imaginary. So although every human being must deal with this impossibility – and it is exactly this confrontation that is the condition for a proper desire, hence the 'ethics of psychoanalysis'! (Lacan 1992) – the obsessional evades his desire by 'choosing' imaginary solutions. His efforts to shy away are a defence. They are aimed at controlling: controlling the other, as well as himself. This accounts for the very strong ego of the obsessional. 'Yes, it is behind this ego, which certain analysts choose to strengthen still more, that the neurotic hides the castration he denies' (Lacan 2006: 700). It also accounts for many of his obsessional practices (rituals) of control. One way of controlling the anxiety-provoking uncertainty is by turning the desire of another person into a demand – that is, something which can be responded to in a clear-cut manner. This may elucidate the mania for organization, the sense of duty, and the neatness of the obsessional.

Whereas Lacan formalizes fantasy by the formula $\$ \lozenge a$, he formalizes neurosis as $\$ \lozenge D$. The neurotic is not a subject whose fantasy relates him to the object (*a*) of his desire but to a Demand that he must comply with. This formula ($\$ \lozenge D$) is also the matheme that Lacan uses to formalize the drive, in which the subject of desire fades due to the insistence of a persisting demand.

'The drive is what becomes of demand when the subject vanishes from it' (Lacan 2006: 692). So the fantasy of a neurotic is reduced to the level of drives. 'Indeed, the neurotic, whether hysteric, obsessive, or, more radically, phobic, is the one who identifies the Other's lack with the Other's demand . . . Consequently, the Other's demand takes on the function of the object in the neurotic's fantasy – that is, his fantasy (my formulas make it possible to realize this immediately) is reduced to the drive: ($\$ \lozenge D$)' (Lacan 2006: 698). This may not surprise us, as it is the lack of a sufficient symbolic identity (of a position in the symbolic order that carries the person and is the ground for a steady relationship to others) that causes the neurotic to find his support in the imaginary (the imaginary is for Lacan also the realm of the libidinal). The imaginary is characterized by dual relations, by the aggressivity and rivalry of ego and opponent. This accounts for the obsessional's attack of authorities. He feels himself to be the victim of an 'imaginary castration': the 'other' has stolen the enjoyment from him. This enjoyment would still have been attainable if the law had not been pronounced. He remains guided by his unconscious fantasy (of full enjoyment).

Psychosis

Lacan defines the psychotic position by the operation of foreclosure. Foreclosure is Lacan's translation of Freud's term *Verwerfung* – along with negation (*Verneinung*) and repression (*Verdrängung*) one of the defence mechanisms Freud distinguishes. In 'On a Question Prior to any Possible Treatment of Psychosis', Lacan writes:

> I will thus take *Verwerfung* to be 'foreclosure' of the signifier. At the point at which the Name-of-the-Father is summoned – and we shall see how – a pure and simple hole may thus answer in the Other; due to the lack of the metaphoric effect, this hole will give rise to a corresponding hole in the place of phallic signification.
>
> (Lacan 2006: 466)

In foreclosure, the ('phallic') signifier that subjects a person to the law is rejected. Usually, the psychotic structure results from a malfunction of the Oedipus complex, in which the child (either a boy or girl) identifies with the name-of-the-Father, which puts it in the symbolic realm. Simply put: because the child identifies itself in the symbolic (as a signifier), it develops a proper desire.

If this identification fails (is 'foreclosed'), the subject of desire can develop delusions and hallucinations. In an auditory hallucination such as the hearing of voices, what is foreclosed in the symbolic (for instance, an authoritative voice imposing a rule) returns in the real. The failure of identification in the symbolic can also lead to a 'suffocation' of the subject of desire in the imaginary relations between its ego and the (illusory) images it pursues. These dualistic relations are then not mediated by the third instance of the law. It is the lack of the Name-of-the-Father that 'sets off a cascade of reworkings of the signifier from which the growing disaster of the imaginary proceeds, until the level is reached at which signifier and signified stabilize in a delusional metaphor' (Lacan 2006: 481). In psychosis, there is an 'inadequacy of the metaphoric effect', of substituting one signifier for another, which leads to a 'hypostatization' of language and a limitation of signifying effects. For it is 'the metaphoric structure, indicating that it is in the substitution of signifier for signifier that an effect of signification is produced that is poetic or creative' (Lacan 2006: 429).[5] A psychotic may 'hypostatize' language, as well as the object that he imagines to be for an other, and subsequently feel threatened by it (for instance, 'I am being looked at' turns into 'I am the object of their pursuit'). A psychotic *knows* what he is: the firm belief and unshakeable convictions of the psychotic, taking shape in the immediate reality of the hallucinations and delusions. As the psychotic is insufficiently subjected to the law, he knows of no lack (of knowledge, or of being: as in delusions of grandeur), nor uncertainty.[6]

Perversion

> What is perversion? It is not simply an aberration in relation to social criteria, an anomaly contrary to good morals, although this register is not absent, nor is it an atypicality according to natural criteria, namely that it more or less derogates from the reproductive finality of the sexual union. It is something else in its very structure.
>
> (Lacan 1988a: 221)

Lacan does not, as Freud does, define perversion in relation to the supposed mature position of sexual activity in heterosexual genital sexuality. His more philosophical stance allows him to discriminate perverse acts from perversion as a *structure*, as a position in relation to the law. Perversion is a disavowal (Freud's *Verleugnung*) of the law – and not of the biologically grounded moral goal of heterosexual copulation. This shows once more that for Lacan our basic determinations come from our symbolical, unconscious position (for the greater part laid down in the castration complex) and not from nature (biology). In perversion, the law is not a massive and unshakeable ordering (as for the neurotic) but something that can be played with; there is both recognition and disavowal of the law that causes desire. The subject recognizes the law while at the same time stressing its arbitrariness, so that the object is both a genuine object of desire and nothing more than an arbitrary construction.

The (virtual) perverse structure may actualize in perverse acts. What defines such acts is that the play with the conventions and rules is *without sense of guilt*. In fetishism, the (perverse) subject of desire projects so much of itself into the fetish-object (its fantasy) that it is perceived as something that can cover up the lack. The fetish is a symbolic substitute for the 'imaginary plenitude'. In the perverse acts of exhibitionism and voyeurism, the (perverse) subject of desire plays with another person the game of being the object of vision for the other, or being itself the one who is looking. It should be noted that for an exhibitionist or a voyeur, enjoyment is sustained by the fantasy of an 'audience' (the regard of the other). Enjoyment increases due to the fact that someone could suddenly enter the scene: an exhibitionist 'expects' someone to see him, and the voyeur enjoys the possibility that he might get caught (so that the enjoyment involved is not pleasure). Perverts are playing with the limit to the extreme. In the perverse acts of sadism and masochism, the subject actualizes a fantasmatic scene (which for the neurotic remains latent, hidden) in which it is either the object of enjoyment for the other (the passive role) or the master who is in control (active role). In perverse acts, the subject plays with the normal conception of itself and tries to accentuate this conception to the limit. Both within the field of the scopic drive (voyeurism/exhibitionism) and of the invocatory drive (sadism/masochism), the subject of desire plays out the fantasy of being an object for the other. A well-known example of this outside the domain of perverse (sexual) acts is that of a person turning himself into an instrument for the execution of the orders of a 'higher order' (let's say some system or regime whose rules he must obey). The pervert turns himself into an object and seems to 'sacrifice' himself for the big other, while at the same time he is enjoying this position of being an instrument.

As the perverse subject turns itself into an object, the formula that Lacan provides of perversion is the formula of fantasy written the other way around: $a \lozenge \$$. In perversion, the subject is itself an object for a 'bigger' subject (the dominans, the master, the state, a moral good). This inversion of the matheme of fantasy draws our attention to the close connection between fantasy and perversion. In fantasy, we will find features of perverse acts, like playing with positions, and turning oneself into an object. This perversion of fantasy is nevertheless *not a matter of acts*.

Sex without acts: the perverse structure of fantasy

Fantasy is the medium of the split subject of desire, a subject constituted through the 'primal repression' of its entrance into the world of language, which is structurally incomplete so that it is impossible to say 'the truth about the truth'. As such, fantasy is inevitably related to the neurotic structure. 'From the moment he speaks, from that precise moment and not before, I understand that there is repression' (Lacan 1999: 53). Although connected to the neurotic structure, fantasy as a result of 'primary repression' is not a pathological or merely imaginary compensation as is the case for the neurotic symptoms resulting from 'secondary repression'.

To understand fantasy as the primordial medium as I present it here, we must learn to see how it functions as a manner to regain a form of enjoyment that is not the 'masturbatory enjoyment' of the neurotic who secretly and isolated transgresses the law that he so much clings to (who loses himself in the pleasure principle, cut off from the reality principle). And it is neither a form of enjoyment that defies – as perverse acts do – the laws that define our socio-symbolic reality. Fantasy as a primordial medium organizes enjoyment within the realm of the law and signification, an enjoyment that is not the pathological signification and enjoyment of symptoms. This fantasy-enjoyment is what Lacan names surplus-enjoyment (I will therefore end my discussion of Lacan's theory of fantasy with that notion; see Chapter 6, §6.2).

Reality itself is not saved from enjoyment. Thus Lacan undermines Freud's notion of fantasy that draws a strict line between the two principles of mental functioning (his so-called 'central usage'). Although he acknowledges the existence of such a strict distinction in Freud's (1911) 'Formulations on the Two Principles of Mental Functioning', for Lacan even in a simple hallucination, as the hallucination of food by someone who is hungry, there is more at stake than the making present of an object of need, namely desire. The hallucinative images not only function according to the pleasure principle, but also to the reality principle, as they express the unconscious subject of desire and its signification.

> One can argue over each case, but it is absolutely essential to map the dimension of signification in every hallucination if we are to grasp what the pleasure principle means. It is from the point at which the subject desires that the connotation of reality is given in hallucination. And if Freud contrasts the reality principle with the pleasure principle, it is precisely in so far as reality is defined as desexualized.
>
> (Lacan 1998b: 155)

The existence of two principles of mental functioning does not imply a strict opposition of reality and illusion. Fantasy as the domain of the pleasure principle isolated from reality testing is too narrow. 'Reality isn't just there so that we bump our heads up against the false paths along which the functioning of the pleasure principle leads us. In truth, we make reality out of pleasure' (Lacan 1992: 225).[7]

For Lacan, the drive is already operating at the level of language.

> Freud tells us repeatedly that sublimation [one of the four vicissitudes of the drive] is also satisfaction of the drive, whereas it is

> *zielgehemmt*, inhibited as to its aim – it does not attain it. Sublimation is nonetheless satisfaction of the drive, without repression. In other words – for the moment, I am not fucking, I am talking to you. Well! I can have exactly the same satisfaction as if I were fucking. That's what it means. Indeed, it raises the question of whether in fact I am not fucking at this moment . . . the use of the function of the drive has for me no other purpose than to put in question what is meant by satisfaction.
>
> (Lacan 1998b: 166)

The difficult stake of psychoanalysis is to see how enjoyment works in our 'normal' experience of reality, how sexuality that is not a matter of sexual acts works, for 'psychoanalysis has no other pertinence than as the clinic of sexuality' (Brousse 2007: 251). Fantasy is simultaneously sublimation and satisfaction of the drive. It organizes surplus-enjoyment in reality.

The most general characteristic of the perverse position is the ambiguity or 'double talk' towards castration: one does, and does not recognize the lack. The perverse structure of fantasy is that it searches for enjoyment after castration and recognition of the law. It aims for enjoyment not via (neurotic) fantasizing, (perverse) acts, or (psychotic) acting out, but via a medium, a mediating apparatus. Lacan's parallel of fucking and talking indicates that he considers such an apparatus of *jouissance* first of all operating in language (enjoyment in the signifier).

> 'Reality is approached with apparatuses of jouissance'.[8] That is another formulation I am proposing to you, as long as we focus, of course, on the fact that there's no other apparatus than language.
>
> (Lacan 1999: 55)[9]

5.2 Our fantasmatic condition

The double bind of fantasy

We cannot avoid staging our desire, and therefore only have access to the products of fantasy and not to the 'thing itself'. This is the 'transcendental structure' of desire; it is the condition of our being as subjects of desire. Fantasy catches us in a tricky situation. On the one hand, we 'naturally' assume that something corresponds to everything we strive and long for. For if I think that my partner is nothing more than only one of the many possible objects of my desire – a male desire that by its transcendental structure necessarily aims at some female object – the whole sublimated world of our love relationship falls apart. I necessarily assume that there is 'something special' in her (for me). This 'special thing' is what Lacan calls the agalma or the *object a*. Desire is driven by such 'special things', and therefore it always is 'deformed' or subjectivized by means of someone's fantasy. However, we are lured by it if we take this fantasy as a reality. 'But the object of desire, in the usual sense, is either a fantasy that is in reality the support of desire, or a lure' (Lacan 1998b: 186). On the other hand, we will never have access to the 'real object' as supposed to be present 'behind' our fantasmatic representation. If we try to get at the real, the fantasy that supports our desire may evaporate, and we lose the object that we were trying to get at. This is the 'double bind' of fantasy.

There is no pure desire, and this fact is not necessarily 'pathological' (Žižek 1998). The subject of desire has no unmediated relation to its 'true' or 'real' object. At the *phenomenological* level (the level of appearances), the *object a* of desire is always made present by the screen of fantasy. At the *noumenal* level (as it is 'in itself'), the *object a* of desire is an absence. This double bind is desire itself, its (subversive) dialectic.

To use the Lacanian distinction between the (imaginary) ego and the (symbolic) subject, one could say that the *ego-object* is our necessary illusion. Lacanian psychoanalysis can be seen as a 'logic of this illusion', as an analysis of the way in which we are always already caught in a dialectic of the (conscious) self and the (unconscious) other (in ourselves), of what can be mirrored (of ourselves) and what cannot. Its stake is the continuous subversion of the ego's illusions, without believing that those illusions can be fully eliminated. There always remains an 'unavoidable illusion', which is the fantasmatic construction of the object of desire (the scheme).

Traversing the fantasy?

Like the 'transitional object' is 'the shred of blanket or beloved chard the child's lips or hands never stop touching' (Lacan 2006: 689), fantasy frames the object that keeps us 'engaged' in reality. Fantasy functions as a subjective element in 'objective reality'; it is 'subjective-objective' (cf. Žižek 1999a: 313).[10] This fantasmatic aspect cannot and should not be fully raised. Therefore, psychoanalytical therapy is not about eliminating, but about transforming fantasy. More so, to deny being a subject of desire results not in autonomous freedom but in pathology. A 'Freudian' psychoanalyst does not try to liberate her patient from so-called 'unrealistic fantasies'. Let's say that my unconscious fantasy in writing this work is to establish myself as a great philosopher. My psychoanalyst would subsequently not try to show me that this is an unrealistic fantasy and that I also can be happy and satisfied when writing this work helps me to find a job as a scholar, etc. It is not simply reality that takes the measure of my fantasies (the reality principle). It is also the other way around: it is fantasy that *sustains* our reality: we make 'reality out of pleasure'. For the fantasies that might motivate my writing are also what create a valuable reality for me. Because we 'live' our fantasies, dreamlike elements penetrate our 'alert life'.[11]

Where fantasies are not (creatively) moulding but hindering the life of the analysand, therapy is an option. What first of all is at stake in psychoanalytic therapy is that the subject comes to realize *that* he is subjected to a fantasmatic formation of desire. Then the issue becomes recognizing the content of her desires. It is about gaining insight in desire, and not about the elimination of fantasy. From that point on it is a matter of relating differently to the (problematic or pathological) fantasmatic formation of desire. This insight through articulation in 'the structure from which everything gets a meaning for a specific subject' (the fundamental fantasy) is called 'subjective destitution'. The end of analysis consists of a transformation of the subject of desire, a 'destitution' of the place from which it believed or supposed to desire. This transformation often manifests itself as a melancholic depression or a maniacal enthusiasm (Verhaeghe 1994: 203; Verhaeghe 2004: 279), phenomena that indicate a transformation of the subject's relation to the formation of its unconscious desires, to its unconscious enjoyment.[12]

The fundamental fantasy

For both Freud and Lacan, the processes of castration and of separation leave their traces in the subject.[13] Freud speaks of an unconscious fixation to repressed desires. Lacanian theory focuses more on the representatives of those so-called 'unconscious desires', so that repression concerns not strictly a forbidden Oedipal yearning but rather the signifiers that mark the psychic separation from the maternal realm (Gurewich 1999). For Lacan, the pivotal mechanism of repetition is therefore not a repetition of a certain situation that is lost, but of the *sign* that marked that situation and that *became* the situation (Lacan 1966–1967: 15 February 1967). Nasio stresses the importance of the central, repetitive verb in fantasmatic scenes. The verb in the crucial sentence of a fantasy represents the *cut* between the subject and the object, it is a signifier that both separates and reunites the subject and the object (Nasio 1998: 101). Such decisive signifiers determine the fundamental fantasy, the scenes that we (unconsciously) design to re-encounter our lost enjoyment.

This issue shows that the real kernel of psychical reality is (as good as) inseparable from the fundamental fantasy. We may even quote Kant's sayings on the scheme of causality to illuminate the real (unconscious) cause ruling the object-choice.

> The schema of the cause and of causality of a thing in general is the real upon which, whenever it is posited, something else always follows. It therefore consists in the succession of the manifold insofar as it is subjected to a rule.
>
> (Kant 1789/1996: A 144)

In the empirical object of desire we find the fundamental fantasy at work. It is in this sense that we can understand Lacan's saying that (the choice of a particular) woman is the 'symptom' of a man. Similarly, in the returning (conscious) fantasy, 'A child is being beaten' (see Chapter 3, §3.3) there is an unconscious, fundamental fantasy working that turned out to be the masochistic and incestuous fantasy of the girl (for this fantasy concerns primarily, although not only, girls) 'being beaten by the father'. Such a 'real kernel' of someone's fantasmatic life is nevertheless a construction of analysis. The real here indicates the limit of psychoanalytic interpretation, but is still a construct.

The notion of the fundamental fantasy implies a fantasy-formation that will not disappear after accurate analysis and interpretation, but that continues to 'rule' our object choice. In its attempts to articulate the fundamental fantasy, interpretation breaks down to something irreducible. On psychoanalytical interpretation Lacan then concludes:

> It has the effect of bringing out an irreducible signifier . . . What is essential is that he [the subject] should see, beyond this signification, to what signifier – to what irreducible, traumatic, non-meaning – he is, as a subject, subjected . . . This enables us to conceive . . . where the problem of the conversion of fantasy and reality converge, namely in something irreducible, non-sensical, that functions as an originally repressed signifier.
>
> (Lacan 1998b: 250–251)

There is a (libidinal) rest of non-sense, which does not belong to the narrative order. The end of analysis therefore concerns the convergence of fantasy and reality into 'non-sensical' representatives; it concerns 'identification with the symptom' (Solano-Suárez 2007).

> Consequently, it is false to say, as has been said, that interpretation is open to all meanings under the pretext that it is a question only of the connection of a signifier to a signifier, and consequently of an uncontrollable connection. Interpretation is not open to any meaning. This would be to concede to those who rise up against the character of uncertainty in analytic interpretation that, in effect, all interpretations are possible, which is patently absurd. The fact that I have said that the effect of interpretation is to isolate in the subject a kernel, a *kern*, to use Freud's own term, of *non-sense*, does not mean that interpretation is in itself nonsense.
>
> (Lacan 1998b: 249–250)

Although this kernel of non-sense is related to drive fixations, Lacan still describes it in terms of the signifier ('an irreducible signifier'). At that kernel, signification and satisfaction go hand in hand: the notion of 'jouis-sense' expresses this. In his final teachings, Lacan goes beyond the 'classical' psychoanalytical dualism of signification and satisfaction (Miller 2000: 30). Signification is enjoyed, or enjoyment is signification: two possibilities of Lacan's category of the 'sens joui'. 'What else is fantasy in Freud's own work? It is a meaning related to satisfaction. The production of meaning and the production of satisfaction are best conjoined in fantasy' (Miller 1996: 425).

In his seminar of 1969–1970, Lacan gives a (brute) example of this duplicity of signification and satisfaction. What he calls the 'erotic practice' of flagellation has equivalence to the gesture that marks, and to the body as object of enjoyment. This marking of the skin is nothing other than a subject identifying itself as an object of *jouissance*. At the root of fantasy, Lacan says, is the glory of the mark (Lacan 1991: 55).[14] Fantasy furnishes the virtual subject with a 'hard kernel' of identity, by 'marking' it, fixating it. One further example.

In the biblical story of Samson, his hair is his sign of strength: when it is cut he loses his powers. Hair often has the symbolical meaning of strength or the possession of certain powers; it can also be a sign of someone's social position. In all these cases, it is closely associated with someone's identity. Cutting hair subsequently has the meaning of being a sacrifice, or is the sign of mourning. This symbolical meaning of a material piece of the body shows how the subject is closely connected to the (partial) object that it fantasmatically identifies itself with.

This emphasis on the 'enjoyed signification' that fantasy provides must, as Miller explains, make us cautious not to take one's desires for realities and being the slave of one's fantasy. For the most unforgivable error is, says Lacan, that of 'good faith'. What causes the error of 'good faith' is enjoyment: the *sens joui* of fantasy, enjoying the meaning that fantasy provides (Miller 1999b: 11). In 'good faith' one enjoys it to such an extent that fantasy seems to be reality itself.

The sinthome

Lacan considers woman a symptom of man, in the sense that a woman can only ever enter the psychic economy of a man as a fantasy-object (Lacan 1975: 21 January 1975). Fantasy then is the non-pathological condition for giving a concrete (empirical, 'material', actual, particular) content to the transcendental structure of desire. This mediation occurs via (unconscious) desire. However, there is something irreducible in desire, something that makes a symptom more than a pathological formation whose imaginary and symbolic signification we should decipher so that it will disappear (Miller 2007). Woman is not just the symptom of man, it is rather his *sinthome*: that in which the particular 'something' (the mysterious *X*) of his desire is expressed. This 'kernel' of fantasy is beyond interpretation and signification. To grasp the theory of it we must follow the path of the *sinthome*. The *sinthome* opens up a whole new perspective for psychoanalytical research: a symptom is not always the expression of an underlying neurotic desire.

> Lacan coins the *sinthome* to designate the idiosyncratic jouissance of a particular subject.[15] The identification with the symptom is in this respect not a Symbolic or Imaginary one, but a Real identification, functioning as a suppletion (*suppléance*) for the lack of the Other.
>
> (Verhaeghe and Declercq 2002: 69)

In the end, analysis will not eliminate the neurotic structure of the split subject with its 'perverse' fantasmatic mediation. Again: there is no 'pure desire', no absolute subjectivity. The *sinthome* even holds together the consistency of subjectivity. In his 1975–1976 seminar *Le sinthome*, Lacan considers the Oedipus complex as a symptom that keeps everything together (Lacan 1975–1976: 18 November 1975). The Symptom holds the subject together because there is a primal repression that can never be undone (ibid.: 9 December 1975).[16] The *sinthome* is the *condition of subjectivity* (Žižek 1992). This may remind us of Freud's remark that fetishism is not pathological when it is a *condition* for finding enjoyment. Žižek lumps this development in Lacanian theory together in the phrase 'enjoy your symptom!' In the end of our 'self-analysis', we do not reach our 'true self' but a point where it is impossible to distinguish between signifier and signified. Here we reach, Lacan says, the original signifier/signified that means nothing and is just a *sign of arbitrage* (Lacan 1975–1976: 18 November 1975). We could translate this as the self-confirming and performative statement: 'I am this!' This leads to a paradoxical idea of freedom. Dutch psychoanalyst P.C. Kuiper expresses this as follows: 'Man can only experience himself as optimally free, when he is maximally determined by motives. At the peak of his inner freedom he says (like Luther): "I have no other choice"' (Kuiper 1984: 156).

Where Freud gets deadlocked and turns to phylogenetic origins of schemes moulding the drive (see Chapter 2, §2.3.), Lacan develops a theory on the real cause of fantasy that pivots on the notion of the real of *jouissance*. With the notion of the *sinthome* this becomes 'jouis-sense': it goes beyond the dualism of signification and satisfaction. The issue subsequently is to discover how all sorts of significant elements organize satisfaction. So, merely the act of speaking may create a satisfying 'object' (as for instance working in advertising, which is an organization of 'enjoyment in the signifier' as we not only enjoy the material product but also its virtual image). With the *sinthome* Lacan covers Freud's notion of drive-fixations. Where Freud considers fixations to be primal symptoms, in Lacan's view they are of a general nature: 'This is Lacan's final conclusion: *there is no subject without a symptom*' (Verhaeghe and Declercq 2002: 66). Where fantasy seizes the body, it takes root in the real (Assoun 2007: 88).

6

REAL FICTION

Fantasy and the drives

6.1 Passion

Separation

The later Lacan focuses more and more on the libidinal body, that is, on sexuality and the drive, which, 'insofar as it represents sexuality in the unconscious, is never anything but a partial drive' (Lacan 2006: 720). This (bodily) subject is *separated* from the objects of its partial drives, and is not just *alienated* because of the intersubjective character of the human world of language (cf. Laurent 1995: 30).

> During a whole period of his theoretical elaboration, Lacan tries to prop up the life functions of desire. But once he distinguishes the drive from desire, a devaluation of desire occurs, as he emphasizes above all the 'not' on which desire is based. What then becomes essential, on the contrary, is the drive as an activity related to the lost object which produces jouissance, and secondly fantasy. Fantasy and drive move to the center of his theory.
>
> (Miller 1996: 425)

Separation poses an internal limit towards the possibilities of symbolically 'appeasing' desire. It also restricts the early Lacan's 'full speech', wherein the subject is close to the truth of its desire and hence no longer alienated. But the drives don't care about this kind of appeasement or integrity; they want satisfaction. Whereas 'identification is the mode by which desire is satisfied . . . no identification can satisfy the drive' (Miller 1996: 424).[1]

The later Lacan outgrows structuralism with its sole focus on signifying structures, accompanying this shift with an emphasis on *jouissance* and the subject's *separation* thereof.[2] *Jouissance* is a sense of 'original' (or initial) fulfilment of our desires, best exemplified by the mother–child symbiosis – which also shows its enclosing aspects for individual consciousness (like an addict is enclosed in his own world because of the 'shortcut' to enjoyment).

This *jouissance*, the original unity or completeness (prohibited by the father-function), is what we have always already lost. 'Prohibition is the myth of a loss' (Miller 1996: 424). We are not able to find this 'Other half' in its entirety, only partially, by fantasy and the partial drives – that is what Lacan's reading of Plato's myth of completion, put into the mouth of Aristophanes in the *Symposium*, and his own myth of the 'lamella' tells us.

The 'Other half' falls to pieces (of enjoyment)

In contrast to Aristophanes' myth of love as the pursuit of the 'Other half', the subject of desire does not have a complementary part that can deliver it.

> Aristophanes' myth pictures the pursuit of the complement for us in a moving, and misleading, way, by articulating that it is the other, one's sexual other half, that the living being seeks in love. To this mythical representation of the mystery of love, analytic experience substitutes the search by the subject, not of the sexual complement, but of the part of himself, lost forever, that is constituted by the fact that he is only a sexed living being, and that he is no longer immortal.
>
> (Lacan 1998b: 205)

Lacan puts his myth of the 'lamella' (Lacan 1998b: 197–199; Lacan 2006: 717–720) against the myth of Aristophanes. Like an egg (with the perfect shape of continuity of Aristophanes' original people) must break for the new creature to appear, eternal life gets lost with sexual reproduction.

> In considering the sphericity of primordial Man as much as his division, it is the egg that comes to mind and that has thus perhaps been repressed since Plato, given the preeminence granted for centuries to the sphere in a hierarchy of forms sanctioned by the natural sciences (. . .) what the newborn loses is not, as analysts think, its mother, but rather its anatomical complement. Midwives call it the 'afterbirth' [*délivre*]. Now imagine that every time the membranes burst, a phantom – an infinitely more primal form of life, in no ways willing to settle for a duplicate role in some microcosmic world within a world – takes flight through the same passage. Man [*l'Homme*] is made by breaking an egg.
>
> (Lacan 2006: 717)

The 'lamella' is what gets lost every time sexual reproduction leads to new life. 'My lamella represents here the part of a living being that is lost when that being is produced through the straits of sex' (Lacan 2006: 718). What is lost is immortality, for the lamella is, 'like the amoeba in relation to sexed beings, immortal – because it survives any division' (Lacan 1998b: 197).

Lacan connects this immortality, this 'indivisibility' of the living being to libido. He calls the 'lamella' the libido, the pure force of a life that is indestructible (Lacan 1998b: 198). The image of the 'lamella' supplements Aristophanes' myth of 'pure desire' with the notion of the drive. Lacan uses his myth of the lamella that links life to death for his broader theory on sexuality. There is no sexual completion of desire; man does not complete woman, or vice versa. Not even love can bring salvation. For sexuality this implies that 'there is no access to the opposite sex as Other except via the so-called partial drives wherein the subject seeks an object to take the place of the loss of life he has sustained due to the fact that he is sexed' (Lacan 2006: 720).

So it is sexual reproduction that introduces in life a *real* loss, the loss of being One (with the mother, the lover), a loss of continuity. This is not a loss that man can cancel by recovering what has been lost. Our condition as individual beings is limitation, the loss of eternity; sexuality and death are central to it. The myth of the 'lamella' must explain and reconcile 'the two sides of the drive – which, at one and the same time, makes present sexuality in the unconscious and represents, in its essence, death' (Lacan 1998b: 199).

Man can only *retrace* the original plenitude (continuity, *jouissance*) it has lost, without finding it again. This retracing is the (libidinal) path of fantasy. Fantasy is a means to regain pieces of this lost *jouissance* – and thus not only a way to deal with our alienation but also a way to deal with our separation from the object of enjoyment. It seeks to regain the lost *jouissance* in some object: surplus-enjoyment. Fantasy retraces the lost object of desire. As this track is also a libidinal one, at the level of the partial drives this object appears in several guises.[3]

Drives as myths

We have underlined that the drives do not have a natural object in reality; their objects are psychical constructions. The undiluted distinction between reality and imagination hence loses its signification: the representations of the drive are just as much a fictitious reality as a real fiction (Bernet 1996: 182). To clarify this fantasmatic mediation, Lacan accentuates Freud's saying that the drives are actually our myths.

> The drives are our myths, said Freud. This must not be understood as a reference to the unreal. For it is the real that the drives mythify, as myths usually do: here it is the real which creates [*fait*] desire by reproducing therein the relationship of the subject to the lost object.
>
> (Lacan 1996: 418)

As myths tell stories about origins, the subject of the drive 'fantasizes' about its object.

The drive apparently has a 'natural' object; only at first hand it is 'natural'. Considering drives as natural means to fulfil biological needs 'forgets' the fantasmatic element that functions as a screen between man and world. Therefore, Lacan suggests considering libido as the 'surface effect' of a force field rather than as a biologically given force. 'Let us say that it is *qua* surface that it organizes this force field. This conception can be tested by realizing that Freud considered the drive to be structured like a montage' (Lacan 2006: 718). This formation of the object is so original that we seem to have a natural relation to the outside world. It is for that reason that Freud comes to the remarkable conclusion that *original fantasies* appear to be *instinctual* in man. So when Freud asked himself whether there was anything comparable to the 'instinct in animals', he found the equivalent not in the drives (*Triebe*) but in primal fantasies, demonstrating his unwillingness to explain fantasy on biological grounds (Freud 1915b: 195; Freud 1918: 120, fn; Laplanche and Pontalis 1986: 23). Fantasy provides the coordinates for our 'natural' relation to the world. So the woman that attracts me is not my 'sexual other half' but merely appears as such because she fits within the fantasmatic coordinates that direct my drives.

Lacan follows with the thesis that 'there is no sexual relation'. With Freud he shares the idea that the object (*a*) of the drive is actually a matter of our deepest fantasies:

> after the mapping of the subject in relation to the [object] *a*, the experience of the fundamental fantasy becomes the drive.
>
> (Lacan 1998b: 273)

Cut: the object a

Crucial to the logic of fantasy and to the theory of psychoanalysis in general, is the determination of the fantasy-object or *object a* (cf. Lacan 1966–1967: 16 November 1966). The object of central concern to psychoanalysis is simultaneously of the order of the drives and of the order of desire. The best formula for this *object a*, Lacan says in an ambiguous remark, is that the drive moves around it (Lacan 1998b: 168). The *object a* is that from which the organism must separate itself to constitute itself as a subject (Lacan 1998b: 103). In that sense, the *object a* closely relates to the 'lamella', the indestructible force (continuity) the individual being loses with its emergence. Actually, the

> *objects a* are merely its representatives, its figures. The breast – as equivocal, as an element characteristic of the mammiferous organization, the placenta for example – certainly represents that part of himself that the individual loses at birth, and which may serve to symbolize the most profound lost object. I could make the same kind of reference for all the other objects.
>
> (Lacan 1998b: 198)

Rendering Lacan's description of the *object a* in case of the oral drive can be helpful to understand this difficult notion: 'It is not introduced as the original food, it is introduced from the fact that no food will ever satisfy the oral drive, except by circumventing the eternally lacking object' (Lacan 1998b: 180). This explains Freud's statement that the object in the drive is of no importance, is a matter of total indifference (Lacan 1998b: 168). The goal of the partial drives is not to reach this or that object and to consume it. Rather, they must be understood from their *aim*, which is, following Lacan, to perpetually organize forms of enjoyment by constantly circling around the (impossible) object. In case of the oral drive, this ultimate (mythical) object is the breast. 'As far as the oral drive is concerned, for example, it is obvious that it is not a question of food, nor the echo of food, nor the mother's care, but of something that is called the breast' (Lacan 1998b: 168). As such, the *object a* of the drive causes desire. The *object a* is thus the object of the drive and the cause of desire.

Decisive for the *object a* is its element of *cutting* off ('coupure'). Lacan refers to the phallus (here as penis) as a part of the body that manifests the cut in a privileged way. Circumcision testifies to this: a part of the (skin of the) penis is cut off to mark the person's transition to the divine realm. Similarly, the central role of the penis in the child's phallic phase, in which it imagines the penis as something that can be cut off. The tumescence of the penis also contributes to its privileged position as a marker (Lacan 1958–1959: 20 May 1959). In his 1958–1959 seminar called *Desire and its Interpretation*, in which Lacan sets himself the goal of defining fantasy (Lacan 1958–1959: 12 November 1958), he distinguishes a register of the *object a* that concerns the castration complex and the phallus (the 'genital object'; I will discuss the pre-genital objects in the next section). In most cases, Lacan does not use the term phallus as an indication of the penis, but as an exceptional signifier. Unlike the partial objects, the phallus does not 'stimulate' an erogenous part of the subject, but the subject as a whole (it is the object of the 'unified', 'mature' genital drive). It is not a partial object but, as he explains in his text 'The Signification of the Phallus', 'the signifier that is destined to designate meaning effects as a whole' (Lacan 2006: 579). The 'phallic signifier' is the passionate object of the symbolic subject.[4]

For the earlier Lacan, the subject of desire finds its foundations in the Other; for the later Lacan, the subject finds its ground in fantasy. Lacan's notion of the *object a* seems to imply that patriarchal or phallic subjectivation (that makes us a subject of the Society of the Father, of paternalism) does not have a natural privilege for assuming our desire. The *object a* also gives way to other forms of subjectivation. It is not (necessarily) the phallus that must be recognized as the privileged signifier (cf. Butler 1990 and Irigaray 1985, who use mimesis as a critical tool to show that women are something other than the repeated, stereotypical image to which they are reduced). Different, contingent signs can also incorporate this *functioning of the phallus*. Then we are dealing with signs that 'erect' someone as a specific person with a certain symbolic identity. Thus, wearing a brand name such as Nike can help to establish (sustain, support) someone's socio-symbolic identity. Lacan's exposition on the phallus as an *object a* in Seminar 6 is exemplary for this process of supplementing the 'classical' version of Lacanian thought, and transforming it into a more valuable and contemporary version. Then the issue is how people actually 'cut' the law into their existence (or actually into their bodies as in tattooing or in the pathological practice of cutting oneself). For the later Lacan, an important issue concerns the investigation of how humans (re)find a real element at the core of their psychical reality (the *sinthome*).

The cut separating subject and object can be retraced in the central (signifying) element of fantasies, whose nature it is to seek a reunification of subject and object. In the discussion of the fundamental fantasy (see Chapter 5, §5.2), we saw the importance of the central, repetitive verb in fantasmatic scenes, which represents the *cut* between the subject and the object. Like in the fantasy analysed by Laurent (see Chapter 3, §3.3), the verb 'bad boy' contained the master signifier that both separated and reunited the child and its mother. The cut as the determining quality of the *object a* can also be found in a signifying cut that marks the body. History and ethnography sufficiently show that mutilation – separating a part of oneself – is essential to initiation rituals in which man defines his access to a superior dimension. Such mutilations function as an index, they orient desire and change the nature of the person who subjects himself to them (Lacan 1958–1959: 20 May 1959). Therefore, such markings function as the *object a*: they are the real elements of fantasy – cut into the body (or in case of a brand name: put on the body). Tattooing further illustrates this. A tattoo is pivotal to the way someone directs his life, to the way he situates himself to others, etc. It functions as a signifying mark that orients his desire. It is a *real* element that carries the symbolic identity of the subject! (cf. Lacan 1958–1959: 13 May 1959).

6.2 Partial objects

Breast and excrement

Freud already acknowledged that partial objects determine intersubjective relationships ('object-relations'). In his seminar *Desire and its Interpretation*, Lacan introduces the pregenital register of the *object a*, the oral and the anal object, by defining man at the level of material exchange as an animal with two holes: one by which it comes in, and one by which it goes out. Exactly this characteristic makes the pregenital object play its signifying function in fantasy (Lacan 1958–1959: 20 May 1959). On the level of pregenital objects, fantasy is an 'imaginarization' and 'symbolization' of objects that can be cut off from the erogenous zones of the mouth and anus. The infant experiences the breast and the excrements as such objects cut off from its body.

The object of the oral drive is not the breast as a 'material' object, but as a 'psychical' object. Crucial for the oral drive is the enjoyment that went along with the process of feeding. Orally oriented fantasies try to get back some of the subject's lost enjoyment by 'imagining' an object that can 'feed' it. The object thus functions as an 'inexhaustible source' – such as a beloved person who must give everything (s)he has got to the loving subject. In a tedious form, orality expresses itself in the subject's continuous demands to the other who, whatever he does, always fails in his 'duties' – at least: as such it is felt by the subject of (pathological) fantasy. Freud therefore considers the oral phase a 'cannibalistic' phase that seeks to fully include or absorb the other – as fantasy-object ('because I'm so fond of you I want to eat you'). This orality exemplifies all subsequent forms of identification. Both Freud and Lacan diagnose some characteristic of orality: a too strong (imaginary) identification; the undoing of boundaries and differences between the subject and the other, or between a subject and its environment. Feelings of ecstasy would thus have their roots in an imagined reunion with the mother.

Also, the second partial object that both Freud and Lacan acknowledge, the anal object, is already for Freud more than an object of auto-erotic pleasure. In the phase of toilet training, the child's retaining and letting go of its excrements also communicates a message to its caretakers: I comply with your demand or I resist it. The excrements become in this way a first 'gift' to the other. The association with all sorts of objects that can pass for 'gifts' (I give you – or not – something that is precious to me . . . my time, money, attention) expresses the subject's fantasmatic relationship to others.

The voice

The third register of the *object a* in Seminar 6 entails the transition from the symbolic Other to fantasy as the guarantee and support of desire. Lacan elucidates this in the aural domain by means of the invocatory drive and its object: the voice. Also the voice can be an object of the drive. Actually, the voice is an object so captivating that it closely connects to the unconscious. Examples can be found in delusions, when someone perceives an imagined voice (from himself, from another: whose voice is it?) as real. The voice is the subject's *real weight* in discourse, in the formation of the superego: it represents the instance of the Other that manifests itself as real (Lacan 1958–1959: 20 May 1959).

This notion of the voice as an object of the drive goes back to the analysis of psychosis. The delusional person experiences the voice as unmediated: the hearing of a voice is not a matter of imagination but is perceived as real. That's why, Lacan says, for a delusional there is nothing more consistent and existent than the voice itself. As one manifestation of the *object a*, also the voice is an 'object' cut off from the body, as exemplified by the telephone: it drifts far away from the rest of the body. However, the voice in delusion differs completely from the voice we may hear on a telephone: whereas the one is 'massive' the other may be 'empty'. Lacan uses one example, from what he calls 'a kaleidoscope of experiences', to indicate the voice in its mode of vanity, inexistence, and bureaucratic emptiness. Ringing up a company to ask for some service may confront us with a voice that is completely indifferent to what is personal in our demand. Then it does not intervene at the level of the *object a* (Lacan 1958–1959: 20 May 1959), as the *object a* is what we are most intimately connected to.

The voice as an object shows the two extreme possibilities of the fantasy screen that mediates our relation to the *object a*. It may fully screen us off from the personal weight of messages in communication (the bureaucratic mediation of our desire). Or the screen may tumble and let the object intervene directly – too directly – in our self-experience, as a threatening constraint that eliminates our freedom (a psychotic acting upon an inner voice).

The gaze

Both in English and in French, vision is portrayed under two aspects: one masterful, the other subversive. Lacan seems to develop this distinction in his own way. The eye is the specular, Cartesian subject that wants to represent the world in its mind, whereas the gaze introduces an alterity that is impossible for the eye to represent and thus marks the subject's relation to otherness in the field of vision. This perspective introduces desire in the field of vision. Vision is tied to psychological processes; terms such as paranoia, narcissism, and exhibitionism further express this. Vision also has a power to evoke hypnotic fascination. According to Lacan, there is a special relationship between vision and the unconscious.[5] With the invocatory drive, the scopic drive is closest to the experience of the unconscious (Lacan 1998b: 104), 'it is this drive that most completely eludes the term castration' (Lacan 1998b: 78). The gaze of the Other can be so captivating that 'for psychotics, the gaze can sometimes be felt and seen because the screen fails, which is another way of saying that the Oedipus complex fails. In psychosis there is something that shows the subject that the object is not lost' (Quinet 1995: 145).

For a discussion of the fourth partial object, the gaze, I will turn to the part 'Of the gaze as objet petit a' in Lacan's seminar *The Four Fundamental Concepts of Psychoanalysis*. There he states: 'The split between gaze and vision will enable us, you will see, to add the scopic drive to the list of the drives' (Lacan 1998b: 78). Although Freud had written about a scopophilic drive in the *Three Essays on Sexuality*, Lacan adds it – with the invocatory drive – as a new category to the more familiar drives (oral, anal, genital), and centres his discussion of it on the division between eye and gaze.

Our vision, Lacan claims, is animated by desire. The desire in the field of vision, this partial drive, is caused by the split between the eye and the gaze, between representation and otherness. 'The eye and the gaze – this is for us the split in which the drive is manifested at the level of the scopic field' (Lacan 1998b: 73). This dialectic of looking and being looked at, this division of the visual plane makes the subject a split subject. It also makes the desiring subject already an object, an object in the gaze of the Other. The fact that we are seen by the Other turns us into an object. And it is through fantasy that we identify ourselves with the object that we imagine to be in the eyes of the Other. Thus we look with the eyes of the Other (at ourselves): 'The gaze I encounter . . . is, not a seen gaze, but a gaze imagined by me in the field of the Other' (Lacan 1998b: 84).

As especially the scopic drive is so closely related to the unconscious and therefore subject to fantasy, the ultimate correlate of the conscious subject is not a 'true reality' that it must discover or to which it must adapt itself, but an illusion, in which it imagines to have fully reached what it was looking for. The realization of desire in the visual domain implies 'the illusion of the consciousness of seeing oneself see oneself, in which the gaze is elided' (Lacan 1998b: 83). The (self-destructive) goal of consciousness is complete self-objectification. It wants to eliminate all limitations, it wants to see (itself) as it really is, and therefore has to eliminate its own position. 'The aim of "the window of fantasy" is to enable the subject . . . to see himself seeing himself, to fix, in his own field of vision, the gaze of the Other and to "synchronize" his consciousness with it' (Zupančič 1996: 48). It has the structure of love, in which the lover wants to annihilate the distance between himself and his lover, as expressed in the sentence full of desire: 'You never look at me from the place from which I see you' (Lacan 1998b: 103).

6.3 Tracing enjoyment

> Even when you stuff the mouth it is not the food that satisfies it, it is, as one says, the pleasure of the mouth. That is why, in analytic experience, the oral drive is encountered at the final term, in a situation in which it does no more than order the menu.
>
> (Lacan 1998b: 167)

Structures of enjoyment

Desire is always tied to the prohibition of *jouissance* (Miller 1996: 423). Fantasy is a means to regain pieces of this lost *jouissance*. As we earlier distinguished three structures of subjectivity, we can also discriminate between three major forms of enjoyment. First, enjoyment that recognizes the law and that therefore seeks its benefit in an imaginary realm where the law does not count. Second, enjoyment that transgresses the law. And third, enjoyment as a 'playing' with the law. The law, as normative for personal identity, is the measure.

In the first form of enjoyment, the subject holds to it while at the same time acknowledging the rules and customs that prohibit the ('infantile') forms of enjoyment. This situation of conflict will then give rise to the formation of (neurotic) symptoms. Such symptoms are the clearest manifestation of a form of enjoyment based on *repression*: the unacceptable desires are repressed. In spite of this dominance of the law, the subject is so much attached or 'fixated' to the 'forbidden fruits' that its desires find a compromise form of enjoyment in symptoms. Because of the organization of enjoyment within the rule of the (paternal) law, this enjoyment is called phallic; the limit that opens and closes access to the discharge is repression (Nasio 1998: 27).

The second form of enjoyment does not reside in recognition of the law, but in transgressing it. The subject then rejects the normalizing mediation of the law that prescribes how to relate to the other. The subject refuses to be subjected: it immediately realizes its desires. This '*foreclosure*' of the law, the refusal to mediate desire via the law of the Other, also is a collapse of the socio-symbolic order. The 'passage to the act' is a clear example of such a total form of enjoyment that evades the usual mediation of desire via imaginary and symbolic forms: in such an act of rage, the subject loses himself.

The third form of enjoyment is the surplus-enjoyment. Actually, this is the 'first' form of enjoyment, for enjoyment is introduced first of all as surplus-enjoyment (cf. Lacan 1991: 56). Lacan modelled his notion of surplus enjoyment after the Marxian notion of surplus value (cf. Fink 1999: 96; Žižek 1992: 171). In a capitalist system of production, the workman loses the 'fruit' (enjoyment) of his labour: this goes to the capitalist for reinvestments. Similarly, man as subjected to law – that assigns him a limited position – loses enjoyment. Alienation, or the subjection to the chain, causes a separation of what is most valuable to us. However, according to Lacan, the subject can regain some elements of this lost enjoyment after the recognition of the law. This path is not similar to that of neurotic fantasies, as fantasy is not just an 'imaginary reserve' but the primordial (perverse) medium of the desiring subject. By means of fantasy, the subject of desire organizes in reality forms of surplus-enjoyment.

Surplus-enjoyment

At the level of the drives, the subject perpetually circles around the unreachable object in order to obtain satisfaction. At the intersubjective level of speech and desire, the object remains an enigma: each time we try to name it, it slips away. Nevertheless, it is that impossible object which causes desire, the value that the subject of desire seeks and imagines. Lacan shows this by means of another reading of Plato's *Symposium* in his seminar on transference.

At the banquet, Alcibiades tries to explain his love for Socrates. Socrates is a wise man, virtuous, courageous, etc. Yet all these qualities cannot explain Alcibiades' love for Socrates, so in the end he must recognize that there is a *hidden treasure* in Socrates (the 'agalma'), which makes him so desirable. According to Lacan, Alcibiades hallucinates in his speech an object of desire (Schokker and Schokker 2000: 182). This object is what is in Socrates *more than himself*. The *object a* as object of desire is what is in the other more than himself, like a media personality who becomes a 'phenomenon' that 'is bigger than himself' ('in you more than you'; Lacan 1998b: 263–276). Alcibiades hallucinates this object and transfers ('transmits') it to Socrates who carries it, Lacan says, 'in his belly'. The *object a* is that in the other which makes him desirable (or repulsive), the surplus value that we attribute to the other via fantasy, and that transforms the other's being. Therefore, Lacan names the *object a* the 'semblance of being' (Lacan 1999: 84). Slavoj Žižek gives the example of the anti-Semitic fantasy in which the attribution of that which is 'in the Jew more than the Jew himself' transforms the Jew into what he phenomenally is (Žižek 1993: 268).

The *object a* is also the value the subject is seeking in all of his or her activities (Fink 1999: 96). It is a supplementary form of enjoyment that for the subject becomes the object of his desire. Lacan introduces the term *object a* as *surplus-enjoyment* ('plus-de-jouir') for the residue of an impossible satisfaction that fantasy tries to frame (stage). The *object a* is the remains of the enjoyment of the 'lost paradise', that is to say the surplus of enjoyment after the instalment of the law. As the 'production of meaning and the production of satisfaction are best conjoined in fantasy' (Miller), fantasy functions as a screen between the order of desire and of the drives (cf. Žižek 1997: 32), between the order of signification and that of satisfaction; it is the screen by which the desiring subject tries to regain its (lost) object.

The *object a* is thus theorized from different perspectives: that of the drives and that of desire. As a noumenon it is absent from our reality (the lost object), but as a phenomenon it is the 'stuff' to desire. At the phenomenological level, the *object a* is fantasmatic from the beginning. The real object (*a*) is fantasmatic (cf. Žižek 2002: 31–32). This is important to elevate Lacanian theory on fantasy beyond a theory of negativity (wherein we fantasize due to a deficit in satisfaction) and understand that fantasy is the primary form of sublimation, its condition (cf. Assoun 2007: 18). There is not *first* of all a loss and *subsequently* a substitute of this loss in fantasy. Rather, the 'substitution' by means of fantasy itself is 'original': fantasy is the *primary form of sublimation*.

Nasio tells us to 'guard against what would be an exclusive view of object *a* considered as a loss. Object *a* can be theorized in different ways, above all as surplus-of-*jouissance* where far from being a loss it is an accumulated surplus'

(Nasio 1998: 88).[6] So, inevitably, within the rule of law there is a surplus, where fantasy works. As beings of desire we organize our enjoyment through fantasy. Alcibiades' love for Socrates shows this, as 'he is the epitome of desirousness, and a man who pursues jouissance as far as possible' (Lacan 2006: 700) His position shows the (perverse) structure of fantasy – which is to go, within the limits of the law, as far as possible along the path of *jouissance* (playing with the limit to the extreme characterizes perversion).

The notion of the *object a* expresses that being is at the surface, is a semblance. This is why psychoanalysis of fantasy is not a psychology of the imagination, and why Freud says that the drives are our myths. Fantasy reproduces the relationship of the subject to the lost object (Lacan 1996: 418) through the lenses of the ego and the unconscious subject (Chapter 2). An unmediated relation to the real belongs to the realm of the impossible. The condition of desire implies a screen between Self and Other, between subject and object. When this screen fails, reality disintegrates. When we are in a condition of desire – and not outside of it, as in a state of anxiety – we are in a mediated relationship to the real. That is why desire is a remedy for anxiety.

Beyond mimesis

One line of argumentation in this book is that the strict opposition between reality and illusion is too narrow to understand the productive and transcendental function of fantasy. The discussion of the *object a* as the 'semblant of being' in the paragraph above underlines this. Fantasy forces us to think beyond the classical opposites of reality and illusion, depth and surface, being and semblance. It also forces us to think beyond the opposition of law and enjoyment (that is why it has a perverse structure). Human reality is not without enjoyment, and as such it resembles the playing of a game, wherein the following of rules and the organization of pleasure go hand in hand.

Human self-representation clearly shows this 'imaginary' aspect of our reality: like animals, humans also use masks, or some kind of a 'double' to seduce the other sex or to intimidate an adversary. Lacan uses this example of mimicry to show that being comes into play as semblance; 'the lure plays an essential function therefore' (Lacan 1998b: 107). As 'mimicry is no doubt the equivalent of the function, which, in man, is exercised in painting' (Lacan 1998b: 109), Lacan advances to painting to show the role of the imaginary in representation.

Representation is not an imitation (copying) of the 'object as it really is'. Lacan's theory of fantasy takes us beyond the (Platonic) notion of mimesis that has so long dominated Western thought on representation. The example of painting may illuminate this. Lacan's discussion of representation in 'What is a Picture' (Lacan 1998b: 105–119) opposes what Norman Bryson calls the 'natural attitude', an attitude that was dominant in the history of Western vision and painting, and that was led by the ideal of the Essential

Copy that could be attained by an ever more 'natural' reduplication of the world.

> Each 'advance' consists of the removal of a further obstacle between painting and the Essential Copy: which final state is known in advance, through the prefiguration of Universal Visual Experience . . . The goal towards which it moves is the perfect replication of a reality found existing 'out there' already.
>
> (Bryson 1983: 6)

In psychoanalytic theory, there is no reality 'out there' (Reality, the Idea) in which the subject is able to find what it is looking for on the condition that the obstacles are removed. Therefore, Lacan states that the picture 'competes with what Plato designates for us beyond appearance as being the Idea. It is because the picture is the appearance that says it is that which gives the appearance that Plato attacks painting' (Lacan 1998b: 112). What 'gives the appearance' is desire, our (fantasmatic) relation to the *object a*. In the visual field, this 'object' is the gaze of the other. This is exemplified by the well-known phenomenon that in portrait painting, it is almost impossible to represent the gaze.

> Indeed, there is something whose absence can always be observed in a picture – which is not the case in perception. This is the central field, where the separating power of the eye is exercised to the maximum in vision. In every picture, this central field cannot be but absent, and replaced by a hole – a reflection, in short, of the pupil behind which is situated the gaze. Consequently, and in as much as the picture enters into relation to desire, the place of a central screen is always marked.
>
> (Lacan 1998b: 108)

The issue of deceiving the eye ('tromper l'oeil') in painting further illustrates this role of desire. In the classical tale of Zeuxis and Parrhasios told by Pliny, Parrhasios has painted on a wall a veil so lifelike that Zeuxis said: 'Well, and now show us what you have painted behind it'. For Lacan, the tale of Zeuxis and Parrhasios illustrates how the spectator of a painting is deceived. It is the desire to see that causes the spectator to take the appearance for another reality; 'the relation . . . between the painter and the spectator, is a play, a play of *trompe l'oeil*, whatever one says' (Lacan 1998b: 103).

Visual representation it is not a matter of a perfect reduplication. Fantasy is neither a good copy (*eikon*) nor a bad copy (*fantasya*). It does not belong to the order of the copy or mimesis, as that which it aims at, the *object a*, does not have a mirror image. The *object a* is the missing 'thing' in the mirror image: the ultimate Thing of desire that we cannot grasp. 'It is therefore clear why vampires are invisible in the mirror: because they have read Lacan and, consequently, know how to behave – they materialize *object a*, which, by definition, *cannot be mirrored*' (Žižek 1992: 126). The objects that aim and orient desire have no mirror image, no alterity (i.e. they are real). They need fantasy to be productively brought to the surface.

> A common characteristic of these objects as I formulate them is that they have no specular image, in other words, no alterity. This is what allows them to be the 'stuff' or, better put, the lining – without, nevertheless, being the flip side – of the very subject people take to be the subject of consciousness. For this subject, who thinks he can accede to himself by designating himself in the statement, is nothing but such an object. Ask someone with writer's block about the anxiety he experiences, and he will tell you who the turd *is* in his fantasy. It is to this object that cannot be grasped in the mirror that the specular image lends its clothes.
>
> (Lacan 2006: 693)

Fantasy is the 'stuff' of the subject of representation.

Part III

LACAN AND PHILOSOPHY

7

ASSUMING YOUR DESIRE

7.1 Vision and fantasy: Descartes and Lacan

Beyond Cartesian perspectivism

In 1637, Descartes published, along with his *Discourse on Method*, his treatise *Optics*, which was to illustrate his new scientific method. It aimed to provide geometry of vision, in which the study of light would account for human perception of objects. Light, with its refractions and reflections, passes immediately from the object via the lenses of the eye to the retina:

> the light in the bodies we call luminous is nothing other than a certain movement, or very rapid and lively action, which passes to our eyes through the medium of the air and other transparent bodies, just as the movement or resistance of the bodies encountered by a blind man passes to his hand by means of a stick.
>
> (Descartes 1988, Vol. 1: 153)

For Descartes, the full explanation of perception and light will involve more than physiology, for 'it is the soul which sees, not the eye, and it does not see directly, but only by means of the brain' (ibid.: 172; cf. Cottingham 1993: 110). Nevertheless, it is light that is the 'direct touch' between the object and subject of vision (cf. the metaphysics of presence in Chapter 1).

Descartes' philosophy broke with a dominant concept of vision: vision as a resemblance of exterior reality by copying the object's image into the eye. Descartes' physical conception of light as lines overcame many of the problems of this older paradigm of *resemblance*, for example by explaining the 'bending' of light rays by lenses. Vision, for Descartes, occurs when the light that objects 'emit' goes via the senses and nerves to the brain where a representation of the object is made in the mind (this is what Daniel Dennett calls 'the Cartesian Theatre'). In the Cartesian system of vision, *representation* replaced resemblance. From this point on, the modern picturing of the world as representation became possible (Mirzoeff 1999: 43–44). With mathematics at the forefront, the world became measurable and calculable: space became an object of geometrical mapping.

According to intellectual historian Martin Jay, 'Cartesian perspectivism' is the dominant or even totally hegemonic visual model of the modern era. It rests on Renaissance notions of perspective in the visual arts and Cartesian ideas of subjective rationality in philosophy (Jay 1988). In his history of vision in Western culture, Jay situates Lacan as a counterpart of Western philosophical ocularcentrism, a 'centrality of the eye' in which there is an inflation of the role of the eye at the cost of recognizing that of the gaze (Jay 1993: 359). In the modernist extreme of Cartesian perspectivism, all three-dimensional images are analysed into the flatness of the picture-plane.

In his discussion of Cartesian geometry, Lacan observes: 'What is at issue in geometral perspective is simply the mapping of space, not sight' (Lacan 1998b: 86). Lacan distinguishes physiology from 'psychology', or adds the second relation to the first. The rational subject in geometrical space (representation as a matter of rationality and optics) is not without the desiring subject in imaginary space (representation as mediated by fantasy). With his introduction of desire (the gaze) in optics (the eye), Lacan tries to broach the subject of

> what was elided in the geometral relation – the depth of field (. . .) The correlative of the picture, to be situated in the same place as it, that is to say, outside, is the point of the gaze, while that which forms the mediation from the one to the other, that which is between the two, is something of another nature than geometral, optical space, something that plays an exactly reverse role, which operates, not because it can be traversed, but on the contrary because it is opaque – I mean the screen.
>
> (Lacan 1998b: 96)

In a Freudian perspective, vision exceeds the neutral field of optics. In his 'Three Essays on the Theory of Sexuality' (1905), Freud had already introduced the notion of pleasure into the visual field (the pleasure to see and to be seen, in sexual activity). Freud considers vision to be a drive that inevitably exists in an active and a passive form. Besides that, the pleasure to see is right from the outset directed at another person, and not auto-erotic: we find pleasure in looking at the other and in being seen by him or her. Notwithstanding Freud's remarks, one acknowledges the *gaze* as the object of the scopic drive as a partial object – along with the voice – that Lacan adds to the Freudian theory of the drives.

For Lacan also, the drive to see and to be seen involves the other. Also at the level of the scopic drive the subject is split: split between the eye and the gaze (cf. Chapter 6, §6.1). We are looked at by others: other people look at us, judge us, etc. Then Descartes' 'directness' between object and subject is not at all evident. Representation is not unaffected. On the contrary, it is strongly mediated. As we also identify our vision in fantasy, representation is mediated by a screen of fantasy.[1]

The image and the screen

Vision is not neutral and cannot proclaim an objective point of view, as in 'Cartesian perspectivism'. The optical point of view of linear perspective (the eye) does not cover the whole process of sight. Vision not only results from the subject looking, but also from it being an object seen by others. In Lacan's logic of visual representation, the subject of representation both makes the object into an image, and is an object in the picture of the other. The screen is the place where those two processes converge (Lacan 1998b: 91 and 106).

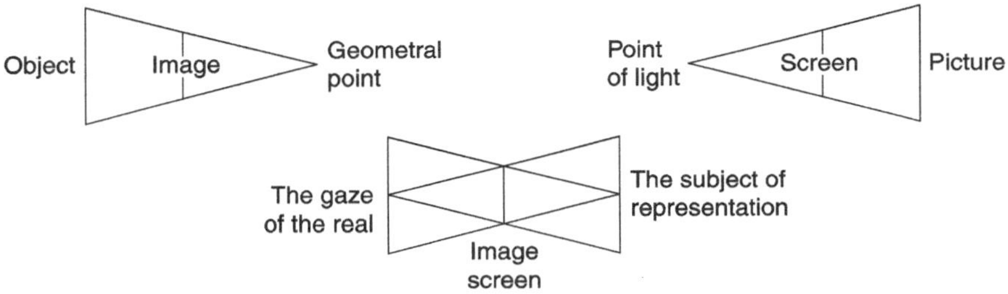

We can also formulate this in the terminology of linear perspective. Vision takes place at the screen that both separates and connects the distance point (the eye) and the vanishing point (the gaze). The vanishing point is the point of alterity, where our vision reaches a limit. It is the point of alterity, the point at the horizon (where 'the other world' begins, where monsters reside). Lacan conceptualizes this as the gaze of the Other (remember the terrifying gaze of Medusa).

> In our relation to things, in so far as this relation is constituted by way of vision, and ordered in the figures of representation, something slips, passes, is transmitted, from stage to stage, and is always to some degree eluded in it – that is what we call the gaze.
>
> (Lacan 1998b: 73)

We try to 'imagine' what we are for the other: that is what fantasy does. Fantasy is the screen where our eye meets the gaze of the other. Norman Bryson analyses this logic via a painting of Raphael, *Marriage of the Virgin*, in which a group of people are depicted with the technique of linear perspective as standing before a temple whose blank opening at the centre manifests the vanishing point from which we seem to be looked at. For him, it is the vanishing point that marks in this painting the installation of a principle of radical alterity, since its gaze returns that of the viewer as its own object. So it is as if something is looking at my looking: a gaze whose position I can never occupy, and whose vista I can imagine only by reversing my own, by inverting the perspective before me, and by imagining my own gaze as the new, palindromic point of disappearance on the horizon (Bryson 1983: 106).

The Self exists in relation to the Other, which breaks up the (self)image and introduces 'another picture' in it (another dimension, like conscience).[2] The question is what kind of object we are in the eyes of the other. Christians see themselves, from a god-like or eternal point of view, as nothing but dust. This identification with the object in the picture as seen by God 'breaks' their imaginary self-image. This shows how the image usually screens us off from a 'real truth' (for living with this truth of being nothing but dust would be unbearable: the usual day-to-day self-image functions as a screen).

Lacan refers to a popular alternative to the use of perspective to illustrate this: anamorphosis. In this system of representation, standing in front of the picture (at the distance point) does not put the spectator 'in line' with the vanishing point. She must put her eyes level with the picture and go to one side or the other to see what the image shows. Thus Hans Holbein's *The Ambassadors* (1519) depicts along with the two powerful figures at court a curious spiral shape that is revealed to be a skull when seen from the correct viewpoint. It hints that the ambassadors too will die and face judgment, despite their worldly power. In Lacanian theory, the anamorphosis illustrates the impossibility to look truth straight in the face (to see things 'as they really are').[3] The image protects us from the truth behind it. Or, in strict psychoanalytic language: every image is a substitute for the truth of castration.

Fantasy as the 'stuff' of the Cartesian subject

The human self is virtual because it exists at the level of representation; it is distanciated from what it is 'in the real'. In particular, the use of language cuts the direct tie with our 'real' (bodily) substance, and with the immediacy of perception and feeling. Because of this rupture with 'nature' (a primary repression), Lacan takes the Cartesian subject as the model of the (virtual) subject of language.

> The unconscious is the sum of the effects of speech on a subject, at the level at which the subject constitutes himself out of the effects of the signifier. This makes it clear that, in the term subject – this is why I referred back to its origin – I am not designating the living substratum needed by this phenomenon of the subject, nor any sort of substance,

> nor any being possessing knowledge in his pathos, his suffering, whether primal or secondary, nor even some incarnated logos, but the Cartesian subject, who appears at the moment when doubt is recognized as certainty.
>
> (Lacan 1998b: 126)

Unlike Freud, Lacan introduces the notion of an *unconscious subject* in psychoanalytic theory. In its 'purest', most formal state, this unconscious subject is the subject of enunciation (the pure subject of the signifier, the 'I') that we must presuppose as the (hollow) self-identity that accompanies our thinking and our speech. For without it there would be no 'person' to which the thoughts and enunciations belong. Due to the structural features of language itself, this subject is indefinable: when we try to determine it, it fades away (doubt remains ineluctable). Lacan makes the '*I think* a mere point of fading' (ibid.: 224).[4]

Lacan's development of the theory of the Cartesian subject leads up to the conclusion that the unity in our self-experience is purely formal, virtual. The 'I' with which I refer to myself does not correspond with some entity in the empirical world. As such, Lacan's development of the Cartesian subject seems to have passed via Kant's theory of the transcendental subject as a formal unity of apperception.[5] Kant describes the transcendental, Cartesian subject as an

> empty representation I, of which one cannot say that it is a concept, but a mere consciousness that accompanies every concept. Through this I, or He, or It (the thing), which thinks, nothing further is represented than a transcendental subject of thoughts = *x*, which is recognized only through the thoughts that are its predicates, and about which, in abstraction, we can never have even the least concept; because of which we therefore turn in a constant circle, since we must always already avail ourselves of the representation of it at all times in order to judge anything about it.
>
> (Kant 1789/1996: A 346)

Kant's 'unity of consciousness' is not part of the world but *a perspective upon it* (Scruton 1983: 56).

Whereas Descartes degrades the role of the imagination, Kant attributes it a substantial position in our 'relation to the object'. For Lacan, the (virtual) perspective that the subject of the unconscious is (the 'I' of the primary repression), is directed by fantasy: the formal perspective is determined by the vicissitudes of a particular libidinal development and by affections. The (unconscious) subject is almost indistinguishable from its fundamental fantasy. Therefore, Lacan concludes with regard to the Cartesian subject of representation:

> Let us say . . . that fantasy is really the 'stuff' of the *I* that is primally repressed.
>
> (Lacan 2006: 691)[6]

7.2 The subject as an object: Kant and Lacan

The abyss of desire: 'What do you want?'

Unconscious signifiers speak through me. This Other in me is like a riddle: Why did I say that, why did I get so angry, why did I take this specific photograph, etc.? In general, Lacan parallels this unconscious, Other side of the Self to a question that another person poses, namely the question, 'What do you want?' The question that fantasy tries to resolve is: 'What am I for the other?' (What does she see in me, what do I mean to him, etc.: Who am I?).

> This is why the Other's question [*la question de l'Autre*] – that comes back to the subject from the place from which he expects an oracular reply – which takes some such form as 'Che Vuoi?,' 'What do you want?,' is the question that best leads the subject to the path of his own desire, assuming that, thanks to the know-how of a partner known as a psychoanalyst, he takes up that question, even without knowing it, in the following form: 'What does he want from me?'
>
> (Lacan 2006: 690)

The Self emerges as an answer to this question.

In general, responding to the question of the Other governs communication. So when the Other is God, we try to find out what we must be, or do, in order to be 'good' in the eyes of God.[7] When the Other is another person in a virtual world on the Internet, I construct my 'imaginary persona' (avatar) not only according to my 'own' desire but also for the other person, in accordance with what he said to me (and with the 'unconscious material in me'). In this process, the subject cannot avoid making itself into an object (like at the most fundamental level it is defined as an object in the formation of the fundamental fantasy). The subject even *must* make itself – or the other – into an object in order to avoid the impossibility of the answer (for can we ever say what we want or who we are, what it is exactly that attracts us?). Objectification is a necessary process to avoid the enigma or the abyss of desire (Žižek 1992: 191). Subjectivation and objectification thus go hand in hand.[8]

> what we call 'subjectivization' [which Žižek describes in an Althusserian context as:] (recognizing oneself in interpellation, assuming an imposed symbolic mandate) is a kind of defense mechanism against an abyss, a gap, which 'is' the subject . . . In the domain of 'pure reason', the subject of pure apperception – $\$$, the *empty* 'I

> think' – necessarily lapses into the transcendental *Schein*, mistaking itself for a 'thinking *substance*', i.e., falsely assuming that, by way of self-consciousness, it has access to itself qua Thing-in-itself . . . the 'lapse' designates the shift from subject into subjectivization: in my capacity as knowing subject, I 'subjectivize' myself by way of recognizing myself as 'person' in the fullness of its content.
>
> (Žižek 1993: 171–172)

It is Kant who teaches us that subjectivity inevitably contains a (transcendental) form of illusion.

The transcendental illusion

For Kant, there are three domains that wrap us up in some sort of illusion. This 'transcendental illusion' is not an accidental or avoidable 'logical illusion' of fallacious judgements and the related 'empirical illusions' of subreption (Caygill 1995: 244). To the contrary, it

> is an illusion that we cannot at all avoid any more than we can avoid the illusion that the sea seems to us higher in the center than at the shore because we see the center through higher light rays than the shore . . . For here we are dealing with a natural and unavoidable illusion that itself rests on subjective principles and foists them on us as objective ones.
>
> (Kant 1789/1996: A 297, A 298)

Some 'subjective principles' make the illusion part of our reality, i.e. 'objective'. Kant describes three domains of the natural dialectic of transcendental illusion wherein we take the subjective conditions of thinking beyond the limits of empirical experience: psychology, cosmology, and theology. Thus we come to pose the following 'objects': the soul, the world as a whole, and God. For the order of psychology this means that we assume the 'I' to be an experiential and substantial thing that is a given fact in reality; while, conversely, it actually is an idea that is indispensable (imperative) for a non-fragmented experience of ourselves. Kant gives an account, or logic, of the 'unavoidable' illusions that those three domains contain, without claiming to remove them.

The same movement of transcendental illusion goes for the barred subject of Lacanian theory – of which the work at hand argues that fantasy is its basic 'fundamental principle'. We necessarily 'fill in' the void of the subject by means of identifications, and this filling of the gap we call 'subjectivation'. We assume that as a person we actually have some 'substantiality', that there is a substance to ourselves. And we necessarily 'imagine' that the object of our desire is the real object of our desire and not merely a fantasmatic construction. This process of giving content to our transcendental form as desiring subjects is the work of fantasy. Lacan expresses the relationship of the empty subject of the signifier to the lost object of satisfaction in his formula of fantasy: $\$ \lozenge a$. Fantasy interfaces the symbolical level and the libidinal level of the *object a* of enjoyment.

The subversive dialectics of desire

In the reality of desire, I imagine how the other is, and subsequently I imagine myself as the object that I am in the eyes of the other. This work of fantasy is not merely a matter of hallucination, as it also constitutes our intersubjective reality. Therefore, it can be called an *interactive hallucination*. As explicitly visible in amorousness or infatuation, it is the interaction with the other/Other that makes the 'hallucination' or 'delirium' (Assoun 2007: 79). This 'hallucinatory' aspect (the transference of fantasy-objects) constitutes libidinous reality between people – recall Lacan's analysis of the 'agalma' in his reading of Plato's *Symposium*.

At the psychical level, reality centres on a psychological transference of 'a special thing'. At the centre of our experience of reality is a fantasmatic aspect ('reality is marginal'), which necessarily takes shape by means of images and signifiers. This fantasmatic core sets out the 'coordinates' of our reality. These unconscious processes also account for the transformations of reality, as well as for the fact that what first appears to be a mere metaphoric construction subsequently may become a new entrance hall to reality.[9]

However, if the desiring subject is to refrain from avoidable illusion (ossification), from turning itself into an object and sticking to that image, the 'answers' that we are (our Self) must continue interacting with the 'riddle' coming from the Other. This pivotal issue is expressed in several manners: against 'frozen metaphors' (Nietzsche 1979), 'against adaptation' (Van Haute 2002), against 'good faith' (Miller 1999b). Lacan examines this 'subversion of the subject', for instance, as the question of the Other causing a hole in our self-satisfied show. The question (the unconscious) keeps on insisting and disturbing.

Besides the object as an image there is another 'object' (*a*) that hinders our full objectivation, that keeps on lacking in our self-image. The difficult issue of fantasy is the double or 'split' association with its object. This brings us again to the double nature of the *object a*. We cannot avoid perceiving it fantasmatically (the specular image lends its clothes to this object that cannot be grasped in the mirror, to use the words of Lacan). If we 'traverse our fantasy', a new one returns. However, we must avoid substantializing the *object a*, the 'value that we are seeking', for this would make dry the dynamics of desire. This might even take us into the realm of pathology, when we take our fantasies for a reality, being without a sufficient form of 'consciousness of the unconscious'. 'Wo Es war, soll Ich werden' is a philosophy of man that is in the end guided by the regulative idea of subjective freedom. We must presume (imagine) such a freedom, although we can never realize it.

7.3 Beauty and nostalgia: Plato and Lacan

Eros and Thanathos

In *Symposium*, Plato states through Agathon that love (Eros) can eliminate alienation, and reunite the divided (individual) human being with its origin (Idea). Through Socrates' account of the theory of the fortune-teller Diotima, Plato explains that Eros is the child of Success and Poverty. In its pursuit of Beauty, it finds itself between Insight and Ignorance. By contrast, the 'Lacanian Eros' is rather a child of language and *jouissance* (cf. Fink 1999). With a reference to Plato's myth, we can say that for Lacan it is language that divides the 'original' experience of being One (*jouissance*); it cuts the human being into two parts, as Zeus did with the original man. Man is both a bodily, libidinal being of 'excitement' (separated from the 'original enjoyment'), and a mental, virtual being of signification (alienated from the 'original meaning'). The result is that psychoanalytic practice is not guided by nostalgic notions:

> The crumbled and crumbling character of that repressed thought is what our everyday experience in psychoanalysis teaches us. Therefore it is a gross and improper mythology to present as the foundation of our experience whatever nostalgia, of a pure and simple pulsation of satisfaction, for a primitive unity.
>
> (Lacan 1966–1967: 18 January 1967; my translation)

At the philosophical plane, this implies that there is no identity of thinking and being, and, Lacan says, there never will be: '*Aufhebung* is one of philosophy's pretty little dreams' (Lacan 1999: 86). When one does assume such a unity between the thinking subject and its object, one gets trapped in what Lacan calls a 'dyadic', imaginary, or 'nostalgic' theory of knowledge. As is the case in Plato's highly influential theory of reminiscence (anamnesis).

> Something of the ability to recognise his natural object, so apparent in animals, is present in man. There is being captured by form, being seized by play, being gripped by the mirage of life. That is what a theoretical, or theorial, or contemplative, or Platonic thought refers to, and it isn't an accident that Plato places reminiscence at the centre of his entire theory of knowledge. The natural object, the harmonic correspondent of the living being, is recognisable because its outline has already been sketched. And for it to have been sketched, it must already have been within the object which is going to join itself to it.

> That is the relation of the dyad. Plato's entire theory of knowledge – Jean Hyppolite won't contradict me – is dyadic.
>
> (Lacan 1988b: 87)

Desire is not a 'mirror of nature'. If one considers it to be so, one is in the dyadic structure of imaginary illusions. Lacan might share Rorty's analysis that philosophy is very capable of constructing such 'pretty little dreams'. Such dreams occur when our fantasy transforms ('substantializes') the perspective from which things are seen (by a subject) into an omnipotent and all-seeing being. This is, according to Lacan, a fantasy permeating Platonism.

> The spectacle of the world, in this sense, appears to us as all-seeing. This is the fantasy to be found in the Platonic perspective of an absolute being to whom is transferred the quality of being all-seeing.
>
> (Lacan 1998b: 75)

Such a Platonism is also working in Cartesian thought: both Heidegger and Lacan diagnose the Cartesian subject as a subject that makes the world into a 'display' (cf. 'The Age of World Picture', Heidegger 1977: 115–154).

Notwithstanding the fact that we have 'lost' the object that satisfied our desires (the original experience of being One, with the Mother), the drives remain attached to those impossible ('pre-subjective') object-experiences of full satisfaction. The drives' excessive nature causes the realization of (full) satisfaction to be at the expense of desire (the conception of the orgasm as 'the little death' says it all). They are essentially death-drives. As the relentless search for lost satisfactions goes along with something 'that goes against life' (Lacan 1991: 51), Eros is bound up to Thanathos. Or, to put it in the words of Marie Bonaparte, 'one of the most constant features of Eros is that he drags his brother Thanathos along behind him' (Bonaparte 1952: 120; also in Durand 1999: 189). Lacan's theory of desire hence continues on the fundamental insights of Freudian theory regarding the inseparability of Eros and Thanathos. Or, it modifies the Freudian binary conception of the drives by viewing the drives that support life, and the drives that aim at death, as two aspects of the same drive (Miller 2000: 20–21). Every drive is, profoundly, a death-drive (Lacan 1998b: 205). When it reaches 'the real thing', the tension in the 'psychic apparatus' is reduced to zero.

In Sophocles' tragedy of the same name, Antigone illustrates this realization of desire as an 'eclipse' of the subject: the result of her 'not giving up on her desire' is that she dies. The final point of desire is the point where desire extinguishes, where the subject of desire annihilates itself and its object. It is the point of (self) sacrifice. Therefore, Lacan states that pure desire is equal to a radical following of the obligation of the Kantian moral law. For Kant, the universal moral law obliges one to treat humanity not merely as a means but as an end in itself, and he thinks that this law should not be limited by any sort of feeling or need whatsoever.

> the moral law which, looked at more closely, is simply desire in its pure state, that very desire that culminates in sacrifice, strictly speaking, of everything that is the object of love in one's human tenderness – I would say, not only in the rejection of the pathological object, but also in its sacrifice and murder. That is why I wrote *Kant avec Sade*.
>
> (Lacan 1998b: 275–276)[10]

The main road to avoid desire's impossible goal is to provide substitute pleasure by means of fantasy, that is, to seek the (surplus) enjoyment of beauty. Fantasy enters in the destructive path of the drives as a protective function: it mediates the subject's excessive striving for the 'real thing' into a subjective desire. I will show this original sublimation by means of fantasy by discussing beauty, as beauty is the name for the *affection that is attached to fantasy*.

The effect of beauty

Plato grounds the desire for 'self-realization' in the reminiscence of Beauty 'seen' by man's psyche before he saw the first light of day as a material being. As our corporeal existence now binds us to the material world and chains our mind, the goal is to free ourselves from the material delimitations. Lacan, who radically rejects all speculative ideas about a higher realm beyond our earthly world, also grounds desire in some sort of reminiscence. He situates this reminiscence that guides our desire in what he calls the real, the real of our past and earliest satisfactions of the different drives. Because those satisfactions that direct our desire are, obviously, not present anymore and are not representable as what they were, they belong to the order of the real as the impossible. Just think of attempts, common enough, to reconstruct a pleasurable event of the past: it is never the same. Therefore, Lacan says, it is via fantasy that we relate ourselves to the real. The lost satisfaction of the drives motivates us to search *scenes* of beauty, not the Platonic ideal forms of Beauty in itself.

Also in Lacanian theory there is an obvious relationship between beauty and desire (cf. 'The Function of the Beautiful'; Lacan 1992: 231–240). Yet not in the Platonic sense: beauty does not fully realize desire itself, as in the Platonic view. Lacan's analysis of Sophocles' tragedy *Antigone* shows this (ibid.: 243–287). According to Lacan, Antigone makes us see the terminal point of desire, and because she does not 'give way to her desire' she radiates beauty. This beauty that the tragedy expresses can lessen our desire; tragedies have a cathartic function. For Lacan, beauty has protective effects: it makes us stop before we might reach the terminal point of our desire.

From this notion of beauty as it functions in tragic desire, one can discern the function of beauty in a broader scope (cf. Rilke 1975: 2, where he says that beauty is the beginning of awesomeness, at which we marvel so that it will not destroy us). When there is no 'happy' terminal point when we try to realize our (excessive) desire, it is only the 'beautiful' substitution of the impossible object that can give some satisfaction. It is, as Lacan says, beauty that can 'dab' or ease our desire. It cannot realize it. It prevents us, by contrast, from the fateful dynamic of 'self-realizing' transgressions by giving a sublime mask to a non-existing object. All most highly valued cultural representations (art, literature, science) focus on such a representation of a non-representable real (cf. Ribettes 1984: 196–197). They try to give a beautiful form to an object that is beyond our (human) limits. In that sense, they all involve artistic sublimation.

Fantasy is the basic form of sublimation (Assoun 2007: 18): a veiling or covering of the impossible object of desire by transforming it. Fantasies are therefore the *media* of the origin of the subject (ibid.: 38). They mediate our performance, representation or impression of who we are, of the major riddles that haunt our existence, of our exposure to the limits of existence. The three questions that for Kant dominate philosophical thinking, 'Who am I?', 'Where am I going?', and 'What can I hope for?', are from a psychoanalytical perspective to a large extend governed by the question 'Where do I come from?' When we reach out to our origin, fantasy is never far away.

APPENDIX

CONSTRUCTING A PICTURE

The 9/11 trauma and its imagination

1 *United 93*

In 2003, the first American film about the terrorist attacks on 9/11 emerged: *United 93* (director Paul Greengrass). It depicts the events that supposedly took place in the fourth airplane that was hijacked on that day: United Airlines flight 93. It starts with the four terrorists praying and making their way to the airport, passing the controls and boarding the plane. There they eventually take over the plane while threatening the passengers with a bomb; they make their way into the cockpit, kill the pilots, and take over the control of the plane. The passengers, after getting notified by their phones of the two planes that hit the Twin Towers and thus understanding that the hijackers are on a suicide mission, eventually attack the terrorists and try to regain control of the cockpit. The last scene of the film shows them struggling in the cockpit before a black screen indicates the crashing of the plane.

As the first film after 9/11 to deal with terrorism, *United 93* was important for establishing the (cinematic) frameworks for dealing with the issue. It departs from the genres of disaster movies (like the 1970s *Airport* films), as well as terrorist films that existed before 9/11. 'This reconfiguring of the disaster movie to the newfound threat of terrorism essentially attempts to reconfigure the 9/11 trauma within established film genres, in *United 93* merging the terrorist film, the docudrama and the disaster movie' (Cettl 2009: 274). The film plays like a raw docudrama wherein attention to authentic sounds, and hand-held in-close camera work brings an immediacy to the film that positions the spectator as a direct witness of the events.

For telling its story, the film uses data from several sources. There were the phone calls that passengers on the flight made to their family members. The film-makers also contacted the family members of the victims so that the actors could play their beloved ones as authentically as possible. They could not use the data from the cockpit voice recorder tape; the transcript was made public only after the film was completed and may in some ways contradict the choices made in the film (for instance, on the fate of the pilots: were they killed immediately, as depicted in the film, or still alive for some time, as the cockpit voice recorder tape seems to suggest). At the end of the film, the makers admit that they only had limited information on what actually took place, and that the film should therefore also be seen as a creative work of the imagination. This is their statement as shown in the film's credits:

> The film portrays events related to the terrorist attack of September 11, 2001. While meticulous research has gone into all aspects of the production, 'United 93' is ultimately a creative work based upon fact, and in dramatizing the story for the screen some characters have been necessarily composited and certain events, dialogue and chronology fictionalized. No assumption should be made that any of the persons, companies or products shown or mentioned in the film have endorsed this production.

Of the traumatic events in the airplane, only some pieces of information are known. In its use of images, scenes, and dialogues, the film synthesizes these pieces into a (meaningful) whole.

However, the film not only brings a visual story departing from mere pieces of information of what actually happened (of the 'object' that it attempts to depict), it also does this for a certain audience (the 'subject' for which the film is made). Thus it affirms the observation made by critical philosophers Horkheimer and Adorno who diagnosed that 'intuitively, Kant foretold what Hollywood consciously put into practice: in the very process of production, images are precensored according to the norm of the understanding, which will later govern their apprehension' (Simmons 1995: 147). The visual story of the film is put together for an audience and considering its 'norm of understanding'. By following these norms, film production already colours the signification that people later attribute to the film. Not just when viewing the film, but already before and also after it, we are constructed as members of an audience: we are exposed to its marketing, as well as drawn into conversations about issues addressed in the film. So 'the presence of an audience is an essential part of the very definition of the medium' (Gripstud 1998: 202).

When one compares the theatrical film *United 93* with its counterpart and competition made for television, *Flight 93* (Peter Markle 2006), the differences in the construction of an audience become clear. With a more limited budget and less intensity, *Flight 93* depicts a story about the same events as that of *United 93*, a story it also tells from the perspective of the victims' families on the ground. As not all of what took place in the airplanes is exactly known, the inevitable use of imagination and of fiction leads to a different 'picture': the dialogues are different, and the interpretation of the sequence of events unfolding is different. But maybe even more significant than the differences in actual content is the remarkable difference in form. *Flight 93* is a much more quiet and calm depiction of the events: it focuses less than *United 93* on the action and heroism of the passengers resisting the terrorists, and of the crisis management of ground control. Instead, it also shows 'passivity', the 'soft' side of inter-human relations, as especially evident in the extensive attention to the dramatic phone calls of passengers saying farewell to their beloved ones.

As a television film, *Flight 93* not only *finds* a different audience, it also *constructs* a different audience. This construction not only results from the imagination of the makers, and their understanding of the norms of the public. It also results from the difference between film as a medium in a theatrical environment and in the home environment (see Phillips 2003: 92). There is the obvious fact that the cinemagoers pay for seeing the film: they are seeking a different environment of experience and are willing to pay for it. They are predisposed to investing something of themselves in the screening of the film; they have certain expectations and are willing to concentrate. When the lights go out, the cinemagoer is separated as a single spectator from the rest of the audience, and can lose himself in the filmic experience. This cinematic experience is much more separated from the rest of our lives than when we watch a film on a television screen; also the sounds and the size of the images contribute to this. The technologies of cinema hold us in a much more powerful grip than that of television: our framework for experience is different.

Both *United 93* and *Flight 93* focus on the heroic stand by the passengers against the terrorists: they are the 'heroes' (a defining signifier) that became enshrined in American popular culture as the sole redemptive act of defiance against the terrorists. Nevertheless, *United 93* focuses much more on activity than *Flight 93*, which also depicts passivity. It is in this position of activity that resides the huge psychological significance of *United 93* – a position only endorsed by its characteristics as a theatrical movie. As Robert Cettl diagnoses in his book on terrorism in American cinema:

> The first significant terrorist film released post-9/11 was a hijack and hostage drama: *United 93*. Where the central set-piece had been the terrorist takeover and the loss of the individual right to self-determination, now the emphasis was on the fight to regain that self-determination through a collective action to stop the terrorist from achieving their planned self-aggrandizement, which post-9/11 had now become equated with suicidal religious martyrdom. *United 93* seized on a moment of resistance to the terrorist agenda on 9/11 and sought to move the terrorist film from the loss of self-determination to the reinstatement of it.
>
> (Cettl 2009: 15)

In this film, the terrorist is 'an object of fear because he represents the theft of control over one's fate and personifies what the protagonists fear. The hijacking scenario and the corresponding fight-back becomes a metaphor for the struggle for self-control, elevated to the struggle for national control' (ibid.: 124). The psychological significance of this cinematic imagination of the trauma of 9/11 is the reinstatement of self-control.

The issue of whether spectatorship is a passive or an active process is an important one in film theory. Nevertheless, I will not go into this extensively but merely quickly delineate the positions. The first position was defended during the 1960s and 1970s in predominantly Marxist and psychoanalytical interpretations of film. They considered the spectator overwhelmed by cinematic mechanisms and ideological effects (the 'apparatus'), so that film was seen as a medium that enforced certain meanings and was apt for changing people's way of thinking. Nowadays, spectatorship is more considered an active process wherein the spectator actively makes meaning in the act of consuming; meaning is constructed by audiences in accordance with certain context-dependent conventions. Despite their differences, both the semiotic and the pragmatic approaches agree that it is through audiences that films become inputs into larger socio-cultural processes (Phillips 2003: 203). The audience that is constructed upholds a certain symbolic order – as it is through the construction of an audience experiencing the reinstatement of self-control that the American spirit is supported.

For documentary films like those on United Airlines flight 93, this construction of an audience depends on the historical data that are available; the way these data are synchronized by the imagination and the ideas of the film-makers; the scenes, dialogues, and characters they 'write'; their budgets and interests; the specific characteristics of the medium, and the particular subjectivity of the spectator in responding to the film screening. Understanding such 'logic of the cinematic imagination' not only helps film theories' efforts of trying to generalize about complexity and significance of film; it also helps understanding who we are.

2 *The Falling Man*

On 9/11, an event took place that was probably the most recorded event in history: the attack on the Twin Towers in New York City. Television channels covered it live; bystanders recorded it with their cameras. One professional photographer was shooting at a fashion show nearby, and after he heard of the events he hurried to the Twin Towers. There he shot an image that soon became the most controversial of that day, and which became known as *The Falling Man*. It shows a man hanging in the air upside down, tranquil and seemingly floating in the air, against the background of the North Tower of the World Trade Center where seconds before he had jumped off in order to escape the devastating heat and smoke of the fires inside. This picture immediately caught the eye of many people who saw it. Right after he had shot his pictures of the unfolding event, the photographer, Richard Drew, hurried to the Associated Press office and was struck by that particular picture.

'It's just that certain "something", that you recognize', he explained later (Singer 2006). Also editors of newspapers were touched by it. One of them clarified the decision to publish it as follows: 'There are some photos in history that are flashpoints, that really kind of get at the truth; there are certain photos that tell the story' (ibid.). Another editor said: 'I felt I was punched in the stomach. It was hard to look at. You feel like it's a private moment, you feel like you're taking away the person's humanity a little bit' (ibid.).

The picture of the falling man showed the real horror of that day. Even during the event, the sight of people jumping was so penetrating that it broke the spectators' sense of watching a vision out of a dream: it was 'the sight of the jumpers that provided the corrective to those who insisted on saying that what they were witnessing was "like a movie", for this was an ending as unimaginable as it was unbearable' (Junod 2003). Immediately after the event, many people considered the picture too horrible to look at, and did not want to be confronted with it. The image was branded distasteful, voyeuristic, and exploitative. The newspapers that had decided to publish it in the September 12 edition received that much angry reaction from their readers that they never published it again. They were forced to defend themselves 'against charges that they exploited a man's death, stripped him of his dignity, invaded his privacy, turned tragedy into leering pornography' (Junod 2003). After its first publication, it almost completely disappeared from newspapers and magazines. It became a 'forbidden picture'. But why did it evoke this kind of response?

Award-winning author on American culture Tom Junod wanted to investigate this question, particularly after having noticed the peculiar reaction towards this image. He heard of statements saying that the people depicted in those pictures did not jump: 'They didn't jump. Nobody jumped. They were forced out, or blown out.' Apparently there was a huge resistance to something that Americans were not familiar with, and to Junod's opinion that resistance centred on Drew's picture. For Junod, it was clear that they died in a way that made Americans feel uncomfortable. He considered it necessary to confront this resistance, and decided to investigate who the falling man could have been. The account of these investigations was published in an essay entitled *The Falling Man* in *Esquire Magazine* in 2003. It was later made into a documentary film, titled *9/11: The Falling Man* by American film-maker Henry Singer. Particularly from these sources I will interpret the public reaction towards Drew's picture.

The resistance towards what is depicted in that notorious picture is indeed a remarkable outcome of Junod's investigations. Significant are the reactions of the family of the person who was initially considered to be the falling man. The wife of this person did not want to be confronted with the image, and considered the suggestion that her husband was 'him' an offence: it would contradict everything that their family stood for; it would be a betrayal of love and faith. Furthermore, the soul of a person committing suicide was damned. Therefore, it would be impossible that he would be the jumper. The reaction of one of the daughters might even be more significant. She was actually traumatized by the idea of her father being the falling man. After a while the family left the house they lived in: the daughter kept seeing visions of her father in the house and kept hearing the whispered suggestions that he died by jumping out a window (Junod 2003). The traumatic idea, the traumatic voice kept on insisting, and penetrated her mind in such an intense and direct manner that she actually had the impression of seeing and hearing it. The documentary tells us that when it turned out that this person was not the man in the picture, things radically changed for the family, and they were 'no longer in a bad way.'

The man in the picture was later identified to be someone else: Jonathan Briley, an employee of a restaurant at the top floor of the North Tower of the World Trade Center. After the events, his brother Timothy went to identify him and recognized him by his shoes of which he took one home and put it in his garage.

> Timothy knew all about the Falling Man. He is a cop in Mount Vernon, New York, and in the week after his brother died, someone had left a September 12 newspaper open in the locker room. He saw the photograph of the Falling Man and, in anger, he refused to look at it again. But he couldn't throw it away. Instead, he stuffed it in the bottom of his locker, where – like the black shoe in his garage – it became permanent.
>
> (Junod 2003)

The traumatic awareness was kept at a distance, at a hidden place, where it became permanent – until the time had come to face it and work it through. What was traumatic was not just the fact that Jonathan Briley was dead, for this was known to his brother already. As in the case of the family of the man that was initially identified on the picture, it seems that what was especially traumatic was the revealing of the manner in which their beloved one had died. This manner, and that is the conclusion Junod reaches, is so much at odds with everything that American culture stands for that Americans do not want to face it, and reject its revealing as being a horrible act of voyeurism.

> In a nation of voyeurs, the desire to face the most disturbing aspects of our most disturbing day was somehow ascribed to voyeurism, as though the jumper's experience, instead of being central to the horror, was tangential to it, a sideshow best forgotten.
>
> (Junod 2003)

The disturbing image should be forgotten because it did not correspond to the image Americans generally have of themselves: it is above all an 'offence' of self-representation.

Peculiar mechanisms of disavowal seem to be at work here. First, there is a disavowal of death. Although everybody knows that many people have died that day, the only pictures that show casualties are rejected. The pictures that circulated abundantly after the event were the heroic ones that propagate that the American spirit shall prevail, even in those times of hardship. Death is only acceptable when it is surrounded by dignity. So the rejection of the image of the falling man seems to be a disavowal of something that is even worse than the loss of life: the real horror of 'a man's death stripped of his dignity'. More unbearable than the loss of life is the loss of humanity. We may vary on Lacan's statement on 'the extent to which the fear of death, the 'absolute Master' – presumed to exist in consciousness by a whole philosophical tradition from Hegel onward – is psychologically subordinate to the narcissistic fear of harm to one's own body' (Lacan 2006: 100). The controversy surrounding the picture of the falling man shows that what we fear more than physical death is dying in an undignified manner. What we fear more than the loss of our body is the loss of our soul. As Junod analyses, the culture of America, a 'nation of voyeurs', is built on this perverse structure of distanciation from the real, while simultaneously taking a glance at its prettification. However, the picture of the falling man smashes this shield of acceptable imagery. This perverse structure nevertheless not only characterizes American but all culture, and shows the central function of the image and the imaginary in it. For as Durand tells us, it is obvious that the inventory of the imaginary is completely oriented by its fundamental inspiration: to escape death and decay (Durand 1999: 391).

What was at stake for Junod was to confront the real horror of that day, the impossible. His investigations try to wiggle a little bit on what is considered the American spirit or soul. They seek to somewhat 'change the coordinates' by which Americans perceive what is most intimate to them, their fundamental fantasy. This is a most difficult endeavour, yet to be appreciated: for it is the confrontation with limits that also provides self-knowledge.

NOTES

INTRODUCTION

1 The title of this Introduction is of course a reference to Winnicott's analysis of the place 'where we most of the time are when we are experiencing life': *The Place Where We Live* (Winnicott 1971: 104).

2 As Lacan considered his work to be a 'return to Freud', Lacanian psychoanalysis is so closely knit to Freudian psychoanalysis that the term Freudo-Lacanian psychoanalysis is justified – and also used by me. Lacan expressed this close and sometimes confusing relationship in 1981 when he constituted the *École de la Cause Freudienne*, saying: 'It is up to you to be Lacanians if you wish; I am Freudian.' This is a reason why this work on fantasy in Lacan starts with the discussion of the theme in Freud's work. And as Lacan's work is more philosophically oriented, it discusses it in the philosophical context and tradition.

1 LOVE AND LANGUAGE

1 As Eric Havelock (1963) shows in his *Preface to Plato*, it is this original presence that allows for the notion of a coherent Self that can produce true knowledge of reality.

2 In the seventeenth century, Descartes and Leibniz formulate theories on innate ideas that are influenced by Plato's theory of recollection. In his *Discourse on Metaphysics*, Leibniz says that he would endorse the doctrine of the Meno (where Plato formulates Meno's paradox of seeking for what one does not know) 'stripped of the myth of pre-existence' (in Kahn 2006: 119). More remotely, recollection is also a precedent for the Kantian distinction between *a priori* knowledge (formal knowledge that does not need empirical evidence for its justification) and *a posteriori* (empirical) knowledge. Today, one can find the legacy of Plato's doctrine in epistemology (the cognitive status of logic and mathematics) and in psychology (innateness in language acquisition: what capacity accounts for babies learning the language of their environment?) (see Kahn 2006).

3 Nevertheless, photo-realism's claim of creating objective images received broad criticism for not recognizing the element of construction in the process of registration.

4 This elevation of the thinking subject reached its height in the philosophy of Hegel. According to Hegel, the Spirit finds its completion (desire finds its fulfilment) in a complete knowledge of itself as it is reflected in the world: *Das absolute Wissen*. Because this 'absolute knowledge' results from a dialectical development of the Spirit throughout history, Hegel criticizes the Romantic notion of an

intuitive knowledge given in 'intellectual vision' (Schelling's *Intellektuelle Anschauung*). Nevertheless, the knowledge of the Spirit is based on recollection. For it is about the inwardizing (*Er-Innerung*; recollection) of the Spirit that was still outwardly manifested (Hegel 1807/1977: 456). The Spirit that gains (full) consciousness of itself is the re-collection of the Spirit that is still exterior in its natural, outward appearances. So the end of Hegelian desire is the dissolution or rising of nature into its *true form*. In the philosophies of Plato and Hegel, the first and the final steps in the metaphysical tradition of anamnesis, mental representations are essentially a reflection of a (transcendent or immanent) 'real reality'. With his 'mirror of nature' thesis, Richard Rorty (1979) expands such a description to the whole of 'traditional' philosophy. Throughout the ages, philosophy would frenetically have tried to position itself as a 'mirror of nature' that reflects the basic structures of reality and studies the laws of reflection itself.

5 In his monumental work on the role of the imaginary in human existence, Gilbert Durand also stresses the relationship between modern subjectivity and the fantastic function. He does not characterize the subject of representation itself as a fantasizing entity, but holds fantasy to be ineradicable from the scientific enterprise (Durand 1999: 381).

6 Freudism does not merely concern Freud's psychoanalytical theories, but psychoanalysis as an event in human knowing in general, in psychopathology, and in culture (Assoun 1990).

7 For a discussion of the difficult notion of representation, and its diverse use, see Perron (2006a).

8 Using the word 'knot' here may already refer us to Lacan's work wherein it plays an important role. Especially the Borromean knot drew his attention: a figure found on the coat of arms of the Borromeo family that consists of three rings, linked in such a way that if any one of them is severed, all three become separated (Evans 1996: 18). In Lacan's seminars of the 1970s, this knot appears several times as a topological figure that illustrates the interdependence of the orders of the real, the imaginary, and the symbolic. In the first part of Chapter 4, I return to the question of what is actually meant in Lacanian theory by the notion of the real.

9 We will see that for Lacan fantasy is the basic form of sublimation.

10 Saussurism is the endeavour to make of linguistics a science in the full sense of the term, discovering and studying necessary laws and their formal expressions. This scientific rationalism opposes the prevailing belief around the turn of the twentieth century that linguistics and semantics could only be historical sciences that would document and record the successive changes of language forms (Bouissac 2003).

11 John Locke was also the first philosopher who doubted, and finally denied, the objectivity of certain elements of representation ('qualities'). He sought to understand the interconnection between representation and knowledge, thereby questioning the objectivity of knowledge. To that end, he distinguished primary qualities that are 'formally objective' (determinations of space and time such as size, form, position, number: the quantitative aspects of objects) from secondary qualities that are 'virtually objective' (the objects' qualities of sense-perception, such as colour, sound, smell). Those secondary qualities are 'impressions' that exist solely in consciousness and not in the things outside us, although an object may possess certain grounds (powers, 'virtutes') for giving us the impression that it is red or blue. But those powers have no necessary resemblance or analogy to the impressions they cause in us. This body of ideas developed by Locke gave an important push to the notion of a 'virtualization of reality'.

12 This conviction makes it adhere the principle of recollection, *anamnesis*.

13 Cognitive linguist George Lakoff says on the conduit metaphor: 'One of the awful things about the conduit metaphor is that it assumes that meaning is objective' (Lakoff 1995: 119).

14 Saussure's theories were criticized for this psychological approach. Some commentators so ardently oppose the anti-realism that goes along with the (methodological – and not necessarily ontological – putting in brackets) of (univocal) reference, that they advance their own preconceived notions in order to keep away from the 'obscure and implausible metaphysics' that supposedly underlies the structuralist theory of language: 'the plausible world view to start with is realism' (Devitt and Sterelny 1987: 220).

15 Because of this 'fixation', Lacan's theory differs from post-structuralist theories on the incessant sliding of signification, as well as from the post-modern (virtual) fluidity of the subject.

16 In the discussion of the transition from metaphysical thinking towards a thinking in terms of mediation (by 'the imagination'), the enduring importance of Plato nowadays is interesting. Plato is, in my opinion, still interesting, not so much as a philosopher describing metaphysical truth, but as a writer; a writer who sublimely articulates man's fundamental metaphysical desire. So the world of Ideas may have faded away, but not the desire for its transcendence. What we are left with of the transcendent object is its 'texture'. So a curious situation arises with Plato. On the one hand, Platonic semantics considers the meaning of thoughts and sentences to exist independent of their linguistic expression (as well as independent of their reference to the reality of the senses). On the other hand, Plato's literary qualities make it odd that he is at the basis of this doctrine. By their very form, the dialogues 'seem to suggest that the situation out of which a given position arises must be considered in any adequate understanding of it' (Hyland 2004: 9); 'the implicit teaching of the dialogues is a notion of finite transcendence' (ibid.). Every philosophical view not only arises out of its existential situation, but is limited to it in the sense that no views claiming 'universal' application are compatible with that teaching. The dialogue is a medium that grounds philosophy in the particular while also attempting to move to the (impossible) universal (cf. Griswold 2008). 'The glimpses of eternity that are offered to us are always embodied in time. The form in itself is thus an acknowledgement of the impossibility of that to which its central characters so often seem to aspire – a condition transcending the multiplicity of the material world . . . the most notorious defining feature of Platonism is expressed by Plato in a self-defeating form' (Blondell 2002: 50). This shift towards philosophy as text is, or should be – as quite some thinkers do not put their money where their mouth is – a decisive issue of contemporary, 'postmetaphyiscal' thought (cf. Habermas 1992).

2 'IMAGINATION' AS MEDIUM

1 According to Castoriadis (1997), this is the primary, though not conventional, meaning of fantasy in Aristotle's work. Also Martha Nussbaum highlights 'phantasia' as the cause of appearance, and focuses the attention in Aristotle's definition of fantasy in *De Anima* on the phrase 'occurs to us'. 'Nussbaum extends the definition: '*phantasia* is the faculty in virtue of which the animal sees his object as an object of a certain sort'. Thus *phantasia* goes beyond just the perception of an image, to the interpretive power of the individual to see that object *as* something: '*Phantasia* is the capability that we have not only to perceive an appearance, but also to say that we see it *as* an appearance of a particular type' (Noel 1997).

2 As Kant speaks in the *Critique of Pure Reason* of 'Einbildungskraft', I use its regular translation as 'imagination'.
3 So already from the beginnings of Western philosophy fantasy seems to be the condition for virtuality. By presenting (virtually) an object that is not immediately present (but 'in absentia'), fantasy sustains reality's virtual character. For a further account of the notion of virtuality, see my book *Interface Fantasy* (Nusselder 2009).
4 As mentioned, Castoriadis gives a different reading of Aristotle. He suggests that the radical notion of a productive imagination is 'repressed' in the interpretation of Aristotle's work, and in the history of philosophy in its entirety, where it only gets full attention in the work of Kant (Castoriadis 1997: 213–245).
5 Elisabeth Roudinesco criticizes interpreters who prefer to use the term 'fantaisie' to the usual 'fantasme' in the translation of Freud's 'Phantasie'. This would erase from Freud's text the development of Lacan's theory of desire (cf. Frank et al. 2004: 174).
6 One could say that in certain psychotic phenomena (e.g. psychotic disintegration: 'this hand does not belong to me'), this unifying activity is diminished. The distinctive feature of the psychotic is therefore his loss of imagination. He cannot symbolize the real, and therefore seems to disintegrate as a person. For the psychotic, the unity in the manifold has gone.
7 Unconscious fantasy reverberates in a troubling manner the Kantian gesture of a transcendental imagination (cf. Assoun 2007: 7). For is Lacan not referring to a similar 'function of the soul' when he refers to the crumbled experience, an experience of disintegration, as in a dream of a fragmented body? 'This fragmented body – another expression I have gotten accepted into the French school's system of theoretical references – is regularly manifested in dreams when the movement of an analysis reaches a certain level of aggressive disintegration of the individual. It then appears in the form of disconnected limbs, or of organs exoscopically represented, growing wings and taking up arms for internal persecutions that the visionary Hieronymus Bosch fixed for all time in painting' (Lacan 2006: 78).
8 In the *Critique of Pure Reason*, Kant expounds this theory in the first chapter of 'The Transcendental Doctrine of the Power of Judgment': 'On the schematism of the pure concepts of the understanding' (Kant 1789/1996: A 137–147). Kant's analysis of schematism has in addition to the *psychological* aspect also epistemological, logical, and methodological aspects.
9 Lacan's 'logic of fantasy' parallels this 'logical' determination of time: as a result of unconscious fantasy, the subject finds each time, repeatedly, the same thing (encounters the same type of partner, acts the same way, etc.): repetition.
10 Despite this composing activity of the subject, Kant rigorously confines reality to the limits of possible experience. The understanding 'anticipates perception' by judging whether the application of the category of reality to certain sensations is legitimate. So although the spatio-temporal world thus appears as on a screen, Kant holds the understanding to have already made a judgement whether there is something real in perception. Judgement whether a perception can be affirmed as a reality comes first. 'Perception is not prior to the category of reality, underwriting it in some way, but requires that the category be given in order to take place' (Caygill 1995: 345). Reality is a pure concept of understanding, a category that affirms the being of something (in time), whether it 'corresponds to a sensation in general' (Kant 1789/1996: A 143).
11 Also in psychoanalysis unconscious fantasy puts a certain schematism in desire, so that certain concepts are applicable to this desire. For instance, someone's unconscious fantasy may lead to the structure of continuously encountering a wrong type of partner, which may lead to the application of the 'concept' of hysteria (a

desire that wants to remain unsatisfied). And observing people who are enjoying their fantasies on the Internet while never being satisfied with what they see – apparently seeking 'that' what one cannot find – leads to the application of the 'concept' of obsessional neurosis (cf. Harpold 1994).

12 It is from this relation between 'pleasure' and the original, lost object that Lacan develops his theory of the *object a*, the object-cause of desire. In the case of the oral drive, this object is the breast; fantasy provides its fantasmatic representations.

13 Lacan calls such an auto-erotic, masturbatory enjoyment that 'serves no purpose' outside itself 'jouissance of the idiot' (Lacan 1999: 81).

14 'In the same way, a nation whose wealth rests on the exploitation of the produce of its soil will set aside certain areas for reservation in their original state and for protection from the changes brought about by civilization (e.g. Yellowstone Park).'

15 The difference between Anglo-Saxon and French 'approaches' in psychoanalysis, leading to different techniques of interpretation, is not less actual today (see Ilahi and Kernberg 2002).

16 Especially Lacanian psychoanalysis holds the (philosophical) view that one cannot 'know' of one's desire without (playing with) the fantasy-scenarios that provide it with an object in the first place. At the same time, Lacanian psychoanalysis is a (therapeutical) practice that deals with the suffering caused by the grip of (unconscious) fantasies on the patient's life. Maybe it should be described as a 'philosophical practice'. For this analysis is, in the end, not guided by the goal to reduce suffering but to gain insight into the truth of one's desires. The reduction of suffering is a possible (but not a necessary) effect of this search for truth. The course and goal of psychoanalysis is not therapeutical but ethical, and in this ethical effort it has therapeutical effects (these ideas are also derived from Pierre-Gilles Guéguen's course on 'Truth and its usages in the teaching of Lacan', Université Paris 8, 2001; see also Lacan's seminar *The Ethics of Psychoanalysis*).

17 However, Freud gives a more concrete form to this philosophical notion of the 'transcendental'. For him, the schemes that mediate the real are not so much universal, rational structures – as the Enlightenment thinker Kant thought – but grounded in (collective) history. The universality Kant attributes to the categories of reason has been the object of discussion and critique, for instance by Wilhelm Dilthey, who considers those categories also to be the outcome of historical processes (De Mul 2004).

3 FRAMEWORKS FOR DESIRE

1 Interestingly, this notion of the Impossible appears in Lacan's theory of the Real via the work of Georges Bataille – whose excessive desires and acts in the secret society 'Acéphale' distressed Lacan (Surya 1987: 256). One reason why Nietzsche is largely absent in Lacan's work is that Lacan's theory of the (unconscious) subject must be situated in the tradition of the rationalistic Cartesian cogito – a rationalism criticized by Nietzsche. Like the Cogito, the subject of the unconscious is a rational machine without body. 'The subject of psychoanalysis, as Lacan puts it, is the Cartesian subject' (Žižek 1992: 68). For Lacan, the subject of representation is split (conscious and unconscious representation). Nietzschean thought rather thinks of the subject in terms of differentiation, and not in terms of split, defence, and repression. The work of Gilles Deleuze propagates this Nietzschean aspiration.

2 It makes man into an excessive, 'crazy' animal (Nietzsche): we always want something more, less, or different from what we need.

3 The decision of James Strachey, the general editor of the *Standard Edition of the Complete Psychological Works of Sigmund Freud*, to translate the German 'Trieb'

as'instinct' received fierce criticism. This would not express the drive as a frontier concept of the somatical and the psychical, and confuse 'Trieb' with instinctual montages in animals.

4 In his 'Three Essays on Sexuality' (1905), Freud illustrates this point by the phenomenon of thumb-sucking. It has no other aim but pleasure and is separate from, but attached to or initially dependent upon, the need for nourishment.

5 See, for instance, the movies on YouTube for an illustration of this experience of a child in front of a mirror. Especially interesting is the documentary 'Svyato' (2005) by Russian filmmaker Viktor Kossakowsky, in which he registers the first time that his two-year-old son Svyato sees himself in a mirror.

6 From a Lacanian perspective, it is from this role of imaginary identification that Sherry Turkle can put forward and illustrate that people can feel so closely related to their 'Second Self' on a computer screen (Turkle 1984, 1995).

7 According to the German biologist Jakob von Uexkull (1864–1944), organisms create their own model of the world, which he names *Umwelt*: an ecological niche created through the interaction with the environment, characterized by certain meaningful aspects of the world for any particular organism (such as in the famous example given by von Uexkull – a specific odour is a carrier of significance for the tick). With this approach, von Uexkull helped establish the field of biosemiotics that studies the production, action, and interpretation of signs in the biological realm. Harvard psychiatrist Arnold Modell gives an example of a human *Umwelt*: 'Let us consider an individual who is fearful and distrustful of others. Let us further imagine that he will selectively perceive only the hostile intent in the other person and deselect and close off any perception of positive feeling. Accordingly, his hostile unconscious intent is communicated to and will be perceived by the other person. This will evoke a correspondingly negative reaction in the other, which the subject will then experience as a confirmation of his original distrust. Our subject has created an environment of anger and distrust. We can conclude that his unconscious intentionality has created an environment derived from his own imagination' (Modell 2006: 106).

8 There is the obvious reference to the concept of the 'body image' in the work of Maurice Merleau-Ponty. Although I do not use and go into this reference, I do make some comments on (transcendental) psychology. The English literature on the psychology of the body has a diversity of terms to express this idea on 'concepts': body image, body scheme, body percept, corporeal awareness of the body, postural model. The following distinction is practical. Body schemes are the sensorial and motorial schemes of organization that are constructed during the development of the body. They allow us to act (such as simultaneously driving and shifting gear in busy traffic, playing with a ball and singing at the same time) without conscious awareness of how we are actually doing that. The body percept, or body image, is our (subjective) sight on our own body and its possibilities. So if someone perceives himself as clumsy, it will be hard to explain how easy it is to drive and shift gear at the same time. In this context of (transcendental) psychology, we could say that Lacan, with his notions of the ideal ego (the narcissistic, imaginary aspect of our self-image) and the ego-ideal (the symbolical aspect of our self-image), focuses on the imaginary and symbolical aspects of the body image. For Freud, as well as for Lacan, the ego is first of all a body-ego.

9 In his 'Three Essays on Sexuality' (1905), Freud investigates sexual perversions as deviant in object (homosexuality or zoophilia) and aim (of finding gratification) with regards to normal (heterosexual) behaviour. Sexual perversions would be a regression to the 'polymorphous perverse disposition' of the infant whose 'sexuality' is not 'under the primacy of the genital zones' but knows of various means of gratification

and is essentially auto-erotic. Zoophilia (sex with animals) would show that the sexual drive has a very large variation in objects and that often and under many circumstances the value of the sexual object is pushed into the background. It indicates (as mentioned in the Introduction to this book) that often the drive itself comes first (as for the Greeks) and the object is of less importance – something that we, moderns, deny by 'excusing' our pulsional activities by the quality of the object itself.

10 This is the basic trouble in the functioning of fantasy: it gives desire its object but can also repudiate desire (I will come back to this issue in the second part of Chapter 5).

11 For some thoughts on the idea that it is the spatial, metaphorical representation of neural events that creates a 'virtual inner space', see Hopkins (2000).

12 The Barbie doll is developed, by psychologists, as an 'aspirational' toy. Barbie offers girls an idealized future self (a world of glamour) and based on all these positive characteristics it is something that children wish for. This shows how we identify, very early, with an image (or second self), how we project ourselves (into the future) and how the signification of this image is governed by all sorts of codified messages.

13 Paul Verhaeghe (1999) introduces a very effective distinction in Lacan's work. He distinguishes the early Lacan who focuses on the symbolic and the imaginary, from the Lacan from Seminar 11 (1964) onward who gives the most attention to the real and the drives (Verhaeghe and Declercq 2002: 61). I use this distinction as it indicates the centrality of Lacan's seminar on the *Four Fundamental Concepts of Psychoanalysis* that I frequently quote.

14 Lacanian theory has been criticized for this 'insatiable' desire that would perfectly suit the capitalistic tendency of ceaselessly more consumption. Nevertheless, one can just as well claim the opposite: awareness of the 'illusory' structure of our desire leads to modesty and austerity. The key notion then is, as in the major philosophies of life, self-knowledge. For Lacan, self-knowledge can only be produced in *interaction* with the other, and not be given by an Other (the analyst, God, the beloved, the producer), or by introspection.

15 Because of this emphasis on 'play' in the logic of fantasy, it may be useful to refer to Winnicott for an articulation of how to deal with a 'return to Freud'. 'The natural thing is playing, and the highly sophisticated twentieth century phenomenon is psychoanalysis. It must be of value to the analyst to be constantly reminded not only of what is owed to Freud but also of what we owe to the natural and universal thing called playing' (Winnicott 1971: 41).

16 Freud describes this in his 'Instincts and Their Vicissitudes' (1915a).

17 Bernard Baas' works (1992, 1998) consider the relation between Lacanian psychoanalysis and (Kantian) phenomenology. His conclusions delineate the fantasy-object as the Kantian intermediary element between the understanding (the intellectual 'empty form') and the sensations (the matter of knowledge). That is, the *object a* is the scheme of desire (Baas 1998: 54–55). Also Žižek considers fantasy (or the fantasy-object) the scheme of desire. 'Fantasy does not simply realize a desire in a hallucinatory way; rather its function is similar to that of Kantian transcendental "schematism": a fantasy constitutes our desire, provides its co-ordinates; that is, literally "teaches us how to desire" . . . it provides a "schema" according to which certain positive objects in reality can function as objects of desire' (Žižek 1997: 7).

18 The translator uses the (Kleinian) term phantasy to translate the French word 'fantasme'. To avoid confusion, I will use the word fantasy instead, as I will do in all texts cited from the *Écrits. A selection*

19 Lacan uses the lozenge for his formula of fantasy: $\$ \lozenge a$. So it is because of fantasy that desire has a 'polymorphous perverse disposition'.

20 I will use both the French word *jouissance* and the English word 'enjoyment'. Remember that 'enjoyment' (increasing tension) is not the same as 'pleasure' (decreasing tension).

4 DEFENCE: FANTASY AS A SCREEN

1 Because Lacan's notion of the real is closely connected to trauma, it is apt for analysing war, as 'war has always been a virtual reality, too traumatic for immediate comprehension' (Der Derian 2009: 10).

2 Art, for instance, deals with this situation. This is expressed in the following comment of an artist who uses Virtual Reality to play with this situation: 'In an environment inhabited by large vessels, the user approaches the unfamiliar territory like a desert island of loneliness. One vessel has imposing eyes following the participant wherever she goes: she comes face to face with what could be her psyche. If she chooses to confront it, she finds herself unable to move, rattled by the world around her, only to awaken back where she came from (the labyrinth), the same, yet somehow different' (Dolinsky 1994).

3 In Chapter 3, we referred to Lacan's enigmatic statement that 'representation's representative in the absolute condition is in its proper place in the unconscious, where it causes desire in accordance with the structure of fantasy' (Lacan 2006: 689).

4 'the subject's "fundamental fantasy," the specific formula which regulates his or her access to *jouissance* (. . .) *Object a* is not what we desire, what we are after, but rather that which sets our desire in motion, the formal frame that confers consistency on our desire. Desire is of course metonymical, it shifts from one object to another; through all its displacements, however, desire nonetheless retains a minimum of formal consistency, a set of fantasmatic features which, when encountered in a positive object, insures that we will come to desire this object. *Object a*, as the cause of desire, is nothing but this formal frame of consistency. In a slightly different way, the same mechanism regulates the subject's falling in love: the automatism of love is set in motion when some contingent, ultimately indifferent (libidinal) object finds itself occupying a pre-given fantasy place. This role of fantasy in the automatic emergence of love hinges on the fact that "there is no sexual relationship," no universal formula or matrix guaranteeing a harmonious sexual relationship with the partner. Because of the lack of this universal formula, every individual has to invent a fantasy of his own, a "private" formula for the sexual relationship; for a man, a relationship with a woman is possible only inasmuch as she fits his formula. The formula of the Wolfman, Freud's famous patient, consisted of "a woman, viewed from behind, on her hands and knees, and washing or cleaning something on the ground in front of her;" the view of a woman in this position automatically gave rise to love' (Žižek 1997: 151).

5 *Jouissance* is a name for this violence or excess of the lost object.

6 Hence one can even use Lacanian thought to strengthen the idea that education takes more than deliberation; man is not 'naturally good' or 'in balance'.

7 There are interesting parallels between Kantian and Lacanian theory. For Kant, the thing-in-itself is both an unknowable X in the external object, and in the subject itself. What Lacan names here, in his scheme of the veil, the 'nothing' that we can only symbolically relate to, is both something in the subject (his 'inner core') as well as the 'beyond' in his outer world ('transcendence', the mysterious X of love).

8 Even the computerized symbol for crying :'-) cannot do without its imaginary origin or resemblance when it depicts a teardrop.

9 Like the film *United 93* does in regards to the trauma of 9/11.

5 MEDIATION: WHERE REALITY AND FANTASY CONVERGE

1 Freud considers castration as the *exit* of the Oedipus complex for the boy only: due to the fear of castration (coming from the father), he denounces the desire for the mother. For the girl, castration is the *entry* into the Oedipus complex: she redirects her libidinal energies away from the mother when she finds out that for both of them the penis is already lacking – for which she blames the mother (cf. Evans 1996: 21). Lacan dissociates himself from this explanation of the castration complex in terms of anatomy. In 'The Signification of the Phallus' he writes: 'It cannot be solved by reducing things to biological data' (Lacan 2006: 575).

2 The 'paternal law' separates the child of the 'maternal realm'. However, it is not necessarily the father who introduces the law, or the mother who is the object of desire. 'Paternal law' and 'maternal realm' are merely (worn-out?) metaphors emanating from the first stage of psychic development. They must describe the process of the constitution of the self, in which it is all about the psychical separation (subjection to the 'paternal law') from an imaginary plenitude ('maternal realm'). The 'paternal law' is hence 'a law which in other cultures might be incarnated in other persons and in other forms' (Laplanche and Pontalis 1986: 31).

3 The ego-psychologists' interpretation of Freud seeks to strengthen the ego. Lacan's interpretation aims at the transformation of fantasmatic fixations to make space for the subject of desire.

4 As hysteria is more often found in women than in men, I use the word 'she' here.

5 The linguist Roman Jakobson (1896–1982) distinguishes two axes of language: the 'vertical' metaphorical axis and the 'horizontal' metonymical axis. Lacan uses Jakobson's work to rethink Freudian theory. For Lacan, metaphor accounts for the 'vertical' process of condensation (*Verdichtung*), which is about the *selection* of linguistic items that allows for substituting one signifier for another. Metonymy accounts for the 'horizontal' process of displacement ('Verschiebung'): the *combination* of one signifier to another signifier.

6 For that reason, the psychotic does not attain truth. Truth (of desire) requires lack of knowledge. However, Lacan also speaks in another way about the psychotic structure, namely as an uncompromising character, and calls himself psychotic in that way. In the version of his lectures in 1975 in the United States (Yale, M.I.T.) that was published in *Scilicet* he states: 'Psychosis is an attempt towards rigor. In that sense, I would say that I am psychotic' (cited in Marini 1992: 244).

7 As Freud's ideas on fantasy cannot be laid down in this duplicity, Lacan apparently turns himself primarily against interpreters of his theory who try to fix the opposition of fantasy and reality as his 'central usage' of fantasy.

8 Translator's note: The French here, *les appareils de la jouissance*, could also be translated as 'jouissance devices'.

9 Nevertheless, one can also find such a functioning of apparatuses of *jouissance* in different, new, formations (cf. Miller 1999a) – the attraction to the virtual worlds of new media, for instance, circles around such 'pieces of enjoyment' (Nusselder 2009). Jean Baudrillard discerns a similar relationship between (technological) media, fantasy, and enjoyment. He considers technical apparatuses to always mediate our enjoyment, but most often fantasy is the mediator. Enjoyment always implies an intermediary manipulation of scenes or of gadgets (Baudrillard 1981: 170–171).

10 Thus it resembles the 'third space' (in between subjective life and objective reality) that Winnicott attributes to transitional phenomena, play, and creativity. 'I have introduced the terms "transitional objects" and "transitional phenomena" for

designation of the intermediate area of experience . . . between the subjective and what can be objectively perceived' (Winnicott 1971: 2–3). 'I am therefore studying the substance of illusion' (ibid.: 3).

11 When we recognize the connection between the intermediary space of fantasy and the transitional space of play, Winnicott's finding is helpful here. 'In playing, the child manipulates external phenomena in the service of the dream and invests chosen external phenomena with dream meaning' (Winnicott 1971: 51). This also goes for the adult: 'Whatever I say about children playing applies to adults as well, only the matter is more difficult to describe when the patient's material appears mainly in terms of verbal communication' (ibid.: 40). Is Lacan not dealing with material that appears mainly 'in terms of verbal communication'?

12 The book *Every Man in this Village is a Liar* in which *Los Angeles Times* reporter Megan. K. Stack reports of her travels to Afghanistan may show us such a 'traversing of the fantasy' outside the psychoanalytical setting (and the book subsequently has the revealing subtitle 'An education in war'). Her travels revealed to her that the war was above all a construction for the Americans to feel themselves strong. She is confronted with feelings of disillusion when this construction no longer works. Similarly, in psychoanalytic therapy the analysand is invited to travel to the point where her (sheltering) fantasies no longer work, so that she may experience or *realize* (beyond rationally knowing) that she is trapped in certain images that control her mental life. The goal of this kind of therapy is to 'traverse the fantasy' and to 'work through' their captivating power and thus to gain a distance towards them. This is a dangerous enterprise, as it requires letting go of one's certainties, confidences, and assurances.

13 Where castration designates the subjection to the 'paternal law', separation rather designates the depriving of the drives' objects and is thus a notion that is more prevalent in Lacan's later work with its focus on the *jouissance* of the body (see Chapter 6, §6.1).

14 One is tempted to translate the word 'marque' as 'brand (name)' instead of 'mark'. This might illuminate the commercial process of 'branding' as operating at the level of enjoyment and status, by pushing the product as an object of fantasy.

15 In a note: '*Sinthome* is an equivocal neologism, combining at least three different signifiers: *symptôme* (symptom), *saint homme* (holy man), *Saint Thomas* (the one who didn't believe the Other – Christ – but went for the Real Thing)' (ibid., p. 80).

16 One can concretize this notion of primal repression, which is the result of entrance into the order of language, by using a different word for this impossible raising, elevation or neutralization. We cannot rectify our sayings, although we often try to do so by saying that 'we did not mean it that way', and thus try to crawl back into a neutral position. But the statement has been made, and functions (unconsciously) as a (symbolic) signifier that defines our (real) position. It is in the gap or rupture in conscious discourse that the unconscious subject of desire is manifested.

6 REAL FICTION: FANTASY AND THE DRIVES

1 Because the drives' dynamics goes beyond the identifications that establish the social order, Žižek can attribute central significance to the excessive character of the drive, the death-drive, in his theoretical struggle against the apathy of small-mindedness and its orientation on happiness (Žižek and Daly 2003).

2 This difference between the order of signification and that of enjoyment is also at the heart of the debate between Derrida and Foucault in the late 1960s. For Derrida, the subject is basically defined at the level of language (through the process of alienation), which is subsumed in the infamous saying that there is

'nothing outside the text'. Foucault considers this a metaphysical position and holds that the deeper meaning of what one says has to do with one's *pratique de jouissance*, one's practice of obtaining jouissance (the process of separation) (Laurent 1995: 34).

3 One of those guises is in new media objects. For 'a restless virtual public increasingly accustomed to high-tech displays for the eye and the ear' (MacDougal 2005: 582) direct communication is also a form of enjoyment – which may be at the expense of the signifying dimension of communication (or signification and enjoyment go hand in hand). For Žižek, the 'decline of symbolic efficiency' is crucial for understanding current subjectivity and society: 'symbolic prohibitive norms are increasingly replaced by imaginary ideals' (Žižek 1999b: 368). Jodi Dean uses these insights to state that this 'decline in symbolic efficiency is a fundamental feature of communicative capitalism' (Dean 2010: 9). Therefore, social media may actually put us in the circuit of the drive. We enjoy our participation in networks of affection. 'Accompanying each repetition, each loop or reversal, is a little nugget of enjoyment. We contribute to the networks as creative producers and vulnerable consumers because we enjoy it' (Dean 2010: 114). 'Networks of affection capture users in the circuits of the drive. The more we contribute, the more extensive our submission. More bluntly put, as we share our opinions and upload our videos, there are more opinions to read and videos to watch and then more responses to craft and elements to mash up' (Dean 2010: 124).

4 However, for Lacan the 'one' object of the genital drive is never detached from the more 'primitive' partial drives. 'The most archaic aspirations of the child are . . . a nucleus that is never completely resolved under some primacy of genitality' (Lacan 1992: 93). So Lacan does not agree with Freud that the genital stage overcomes the 'polymorphous perversity' of the pregenital stages.

5 This is expressed in the literature on this subject. See, for example: Metz (1982), Rose (1986), Mulvey (1989), and Krauss (1993).

6 The objects that arouse a surplus of enigmatic *jouissance* can also have corporal, visual, auditory, olfactory, or tactile forms (cf. Nasio 1998: 95; also Miller 1999a: 23–24). This opens the way for analysing how different media arouse desire.

7 ASSUMING YOUR DESIRE

1 In film studies, this is the 'primary cinematic identification' that is amply described by Christian Metz (1982) and Jean-Louis Baudry (1986). Film theorist Richard Allen describes it as follows: 'the spectator in the cinema "identifies with the camera" and perceives the events that are depicted in the image in the manner of a transcendental subject. That is, the spectator is not simply positioned by the image but assimilates her own vision to that of the camera-eye with limitless powers of vision and sees the world viewed through this eye in a way that appears unmediated' (Allen 1995: 20).

2 This relationship is so fundamental that when we do not identify at all with such virtual perspectives (of others), we are 'outside reality'. The psychopath is an obvious example of someone who does not identify with the way he is being seen by others (being without 'conscience').

3 Anamorphosis also reveals perspective as a visual convention (cf. Mirzoeff 1999: 48–49).

4 Despite its critiques of Cartesian rationality, Lacanian thought could also be considered rationalistic in that it tries to reveal the 'rationale' in the (unconscious) mind: especially in postulating the autonomy of the symbolic it follows a (structuralist) rationalism; later on it tries to develop a 'logic of fantasy'.

5 For Kant, the 'virtual soul' shapes the actual existence of man in the physical world. In his 'On the Form and Principles of the Sensible and the Intelligible Worlds', Kant answers the problem of the incorporate soul existing in the corporate world by designating the soul as having a presence in the world that is not spatial, but virtual (Goodrich 2002).

6 For Descartes, God is the instance that must guarantee the certainty of the knowledge we acquire via a radical and rational method. He must guarantee that the Cogito is not deceived. God is thus the guarantor of a pure knowledge not disturbed by man's subjectivity. From a Lacanian perspective, this God is a fantasy. For Lacan, the true formula of atheism is not God is dead (i.e. without any effect) but God is unconscious. When we realize this, the road is paved for exploring our own unconscious beliefs, for deciphering the subjective element in representation, and thus for radically examining our desire: What is it actually that we want? Similarly, Lacan poses the question: What is it that Descartes wants, what is his desire?

7 Catholic doctrine is as such an institutionalized answer to this particular question. Lacan's position (although sometimes used for defending traditional symbolic structures) nevertheless seems to oppose a 'fixation' or institutionalization of the answer. 'Closure' is not possible – at least, when we want to refrain from the position of self-enclosed delusion, wherein we think we know the answer. We must continue to confront and expound ourselves with the imperfection of the Other and thus with the faultiness of our own answer. The 'hero' of this 'ethics of psychoanalysis' is not the 'subject supposed to know' (the preacher) but the individual of 'tragic ambiguity' (Antigone).

8 Both the words 'subjectivation' and 'subjectivization' are in use. I choose the first one.

9 Žižek speaks of a 'realization of the metaphor: what at first appears as a mere metaphorical simulation, a pale imitation, of the true reality (computer as metaphor of the true brains, etc.) becomes the original paradigm imitated by blood-and-flesh reality (brains follow in an always imperfect way the functioning of the computer, etc.). What we experience as "reality" is constituted by such a reversal: as Lacan puts it, "reality" is always framed by a fantasy, i.e., for something real to be experienced as part of "reality", it must fit the preordained coordinates of our fantasy-space (a sexual act must fit the coordinates of our imagined fantasy-scripts, a brain must fit the functioning of a computer, etc.)' (Žižek 1993: 43–44).

10 For an analysis of this matter, see Bernard Baas (1992).

BIBLIOGRAPHY

Allen, R. (1995) *Projecting Illusion*, Cambridge: Cambridge University Press.

Aristotle (1986) *De Anima*, trans. H. Lawson-Tancred, New York: Penguin Books.

Assoun, P.-L. (1990) *Le freudisme*, Paris: Presses Universitaires de France.

Assoun, P.-L. (2007) *Le fantasme*, Paris: Economica.

Baas, B. (1992) *Le désir pur*, Leuven: Peeters.

Baas, B. (1998) *De la chose à l'objet. Jacques Lacan et la traversée de la phénoménologie*, Leuven: Peeters.

Badiou, A. (2000) *Ethics: An Essay on the Understanding of Evil*, trans. P. Hallward, New York: Verso.

Barthes, R. (1977a) 'Rhetoric of the Image', trans. S. Heath, in *Images, Music, Text*, London: Fontana, 32–51.

Barthes, R. (1977b) 'The Photographic Message', trans. S. Heath, in *Images, Music, Text*, London: Fontana, 15–31.

Barthes, R. (1990) *A Lover's Discourse: Fragments*, trans. R. Howard, London: Penguin Books.

Baudrillard, J. (1981) *Simulacres et Simulation*, Paris: Galilée.

Baudrillard, J. (1988) *Jean Baudrillard: Selected Writings*, trans. M. Poster, Cambridge: Polity Press.

Baudrillard, J. (1996) *The Perfect Crime*, trans. C. Turner, London: Verso.

Baudry, J.-L. (1986) 'The Apparatus: Metapsychological Approaches to the Impression of Reality in the Cinema', in P. Rosen (ed.) *Narrative, Apparatus, Ideology. A Film Theory Reader*, New York: Columbia University Press, 299–317.

Bernet, R. (1996) 'Verbeelding en fantasma', in A. Vergote and P. Moyaert (eds), *Psychoanalyse. De mens en zijn lotgevallen*, Kapellen: DNB/Pelckmans, 171–183.

Blondell, R. (2002) *The Play of Character in Plato's Dialogues*, Cambridge: Cambridge University Press.

Blumenberg, H. (1993) 'Light as a Metaphor for Truth: At the Preliminary Stage of Philosophical Concept Formation', in D.M. Levin (ed.), *Modernity and the Hegemony of Vision*, Berkeley, CA: University of California Press, 30–62.

Bolter, J.D. and Grusin, R. (2000) *Remediation*, Cambridge, MA: MIT Press.

Bonaparte, M. (1952) *Eros, Chronos et Thanatos*, Paris: Presses Universitaires de France.

Bott Spillius, E. (2001) 'Freud and Klein on the Concept of Fantasy', *International Journal of Psychoanalysis*, 82: 361–373.

Bouissac, P. (2003) 'Perspectives on Saussure'. Available online at: http://www9.georgetown.edu/faculty/irvinem/theory/Bouissac-Saussure.html (accessed 3 May 2011).

Brousse, M.-H. (1995) 'The Drive', in R. Feldstein, B. Fink and M. Jaanus (eds), *Reading Seminar 11. Lacan's Four Fundamental Concepts of Psychoanalysis*, Albany, NY: State University of New York Press, 109–117.

Brousse, M.-H. (2007) 'Sexual Position and the End of Analysis', in V. Voruz and B. Wolf (eds), *The Later Lacan: An Introduction*, Albany, NY: State University of New York Press, 251–260.

Bryson, N. (1983) *Vision and Painting: The Logic of the Gaze*, New Haven, CT: Yale University Press.

Butler, J. (1990) *Gender Trouble. Feminism and the Subversion of Identity*, New York: Routledge.

Camassa, G. (1989) 'Phantasia', in J. Ritter and K. Gründer (eds), *Historisches Wörterbuch der Philosophie, Band* 7, Basel: Schwabe & Co., 516–534.

Castoriadis, C. (1997) *World in Fragments. Writings on Politics, Society, Psychoanalysis, and the Imagination*, Stanford, CA: Stanford University Press.

Caygill, H. (1995) *A Kant Dictionary*, Malden, MA: Blackwell.

Cettl, R. (2009) *Terrorism in American Cinema. An Analytical Filmography, 1960–2008*, Jefferson, NC: McFarland & Co.

Cottingham, J. (1993) *A Descartes Dictionary*, Oxford: Blackwell.

Dean, J. (2010) *Blog Theory. Feedback and Capture in the Circuits of Drive*, Cambridge: Polity Press.

De Mul, J. (2004) *The Tragedy of Finitude. Dilthey's Hermeneutics of Life*, New Haven, CT: Yale University Press.

Der Derian, J. (2009) *Virtuous War: Mapping the Military-Industrial-Media-Entertainment Network*, New York: Routledge.

Derrida, J. (1976) *Of Grammatology*, trans. G. Spivak, Baltimore, MD: Johns Hopkins University Press.

Derrida, J. (1978) *Writing and Difference*, trans. A. Bass, London: Routledge & Kegan Paul.

Descartes, R. (1988) *Selected Philosophical Writings*, 2 Vols., J. Cottingham, R. Stoothoff and D. Murdoch (eds), Cambridge: Cambridge University Press.

Devitt, M. and Sterelny, K. (1987) *Language & Reality*, Cambridge, MA: MIT Press.

Doel, M. and Clarke, D. (1999) 'Virtual Worlds. Simulation, Suppletion, S(ed)uction and Simulacra', in M. Crang, P. Crang and J. May (eds), *Virtual Geographies. Bodies, Space and Relations*, London: Routledge, 261–283.

Dolinsky, M. (1994) 'Metaphors'. Available online at: http://www.evl.uic.edu/dolinsky/DG/VP/metaphor.htm (accessed 10 January 2011).

Durand, G. (1999) *The Anthropological Structures of the Imaginary*, trans. M. Sankey and J. Hatten, Brisbane, QLD: Boombana Publications.

Edelman, G.M. (1992) *Bright Air, Brilliant Fire. On the Matter of Mind*, New York: Basic Books.

Edelson, M. (1988) *Psychoanalysis. A Theory in Crisis*, Chicago, IL: University of Chicago Press.

Evans, D. (1996) *An Introductory Dictionary of Lacanian Psychoanalysis*, London: Routledge.

Fink, B. (1995) 'The Real Cause of Repetition', in R. Feldstein, B. Fink and M. Jaanus (eds) *Reading Seminar 11. Lacan's Four Fundamental Concepts of Psychoanalysis*, Albany, NY: State University of New York Press, 223–229.

Fink, B. (1999) *The Lacanian Subject. Between Language and Jouissance*, Princeton, NJ: Princeton University Press.

Frank, A.P., Kittel, H. and Greiner, N. (eds.) (2004) *Ubersetzung-Translation-Traducion: An International Encyclopedia of Translation Studies*, Part 1, Berlin: De Gruyter Verlag.

Freeman, W.J. (1995) 'Chaos in the Brain: Possible Roles in Biological Intelligence', *International Journal of Intelligent Systems*, 10: 71–88.

Freud, S. (1892–1899) 'Extracts from the Fliess Papers', in *The Standard Edition of the Complete Psychological Works of Sigmund Freud*, 24 Vols., ed. and trans. J. Strachey, Oxford: Hogarth Press, 1953–1974 (S.E.), Vol. 1, 175–280.

Freud, S. (1899) 'Screen Memories', S.E., Vol. 3, 303–322.

Freud, S. (1900) 'The Interpretation of Dreams', S.E., Vols. 4–5, 1–625.

Freud, S. (1905) 'Three Essays on the Theory of Sexuality', S.E., Vol. 7, 125–245.

Freud, S. (1908) 'Hysterical Phantasies and their Relation to Bisexuality', S.E., Vol. 9, 159–166.

Freud, S. (1910) 'Leonardo da Vinci and a Memory of His Childhood', S.E., Vol. 11, 57–137.

Freud, S. (1911) 'Formulations on the Two Principles of Mental Functioning', S.E., Vol. 12, 21–226.

Freud, S. (1914) 'On Narcissism: An Introduction', S.E., Vol. 14, 73–102.

Freud, S. (1915a) 'Instincts and Their Vicissitudes', S.E., Vol. 14, 117–140.

Freud, S. (1915b) 'The Unconscious', S.E., Vol. 14, 166–204.

Freud, S. (1917) 'Introductory Lectures on Psychoanalysis Part III', S.E., Vol. 16, 243–463.

Freud, S. (1918) 'From the History of an Infantile Neurosis', S.E., Vol. 17, 7–122.

Freud, S. (1924) 'Neurosis and Psychosis', S.E., Vol. 19, 147–153.

Freud, S. (1925) 'A Note upon the "Mystic Writing Pad"', S.E., Vol. 19, 227–232.

Freud, S. (1927) 'Fetishism', S.E., Vol. 21, 152–157.

Freud, S. (1932) 'My Contact with Josef Popper-Lynkeus', S.E., Vol. 22, 219–224.

Freud, S. (1940) 'Medusa's Head', S.E., Vol. 18, 273–274.

Goodrich, A. (2002) 'Theories of Media: Virtuality'. Available online at: http://csmt.uchicago.edu/glossary2004/virtuality.htm#4 (accessed 13 July 2011).

Gripstud, J. (1998) 'Film Audiences', in J. Hill and P. Church Gibson (eds), *The Oxford Guide to Film Studies*, Oxford: Oxford University Press, 202–211.

Griswold, C.L. (2008) 'Reading and Writing Plato', *Philosophy and Literature*, 32(1): 205–216.

Guéguen, P.-G. (2006) 'The Intimate, the Extimate, and Psychoanalytic Discourse', in J. Clemens and R. Grigg (eds), *Jacques Lacan and the Other Side of Psychoanalysis: Reflections on Seminar XVII*, Durham, NC: Duke University Press, 263–273.

Gurewich, J. (1999) 'The Jouissance of the Other and the Prohibition of Incest: A Lacanian Perspective'. Available online at: http://dept.english.upenn.edu/~ov/1.3/jfg/other.html (accessed 5 April 2011).

Habermas, J. (1992) *Postmetaphysical Thinking: Philosophical Essays*, trans. W.M. Hohengarten, Cambridge, MA: MIT Press.

Harpold, T. (1994) 'Conclusions', in G.P. Landow (ed.), *Hyper/Text/Theory*, Baltimore, MD: Johns Hopkins University Press, 192–210.

Havelock, E. (1963) *Preface to Plato*, Cambridge, MA: Harvard University Press.

Hegel, G.W.F. (1807) *Phenomenology of Spirit*, trans. A. Miller (1977), Oxford: Oxford University Press.

Heidegger, M. (1977) *The Question Concerning Technology and Other Essays*, trans. W. Lovitt, New York: Harper Torchbooks.

Heidegger, M. (1997) *Phenomenological Interpretation of Kant's Critique of Pure Reason*, trans. P. Emad and K. Maly, Bloomington, IN: Indiana University Press.
Hillis, K. (1999) *Digital Sensations. Space, Identity, and Embodiment in Virtual Reality*, Minneapolis, MN: University of Minnesota Press.
Hopkins, J. (2000) 'Psychoanalysis, Metaphor and the Concept of Mind', in M.P. Levine (ed.), *The Analytic Freud. Philosophy and Psychoanalysis*, London: Routledge, 11–35.
Hyland, D. (2004) *Questioning Platonism: Continental Interpretations of Plato*, Albany, NY: State University of New York Press.
Ilahi, M.N. and Kernberg, O.F. (2002) 'New Perspectives from an Overview of the Congress', *International Journal of Psychoanalysis*, 83: 257–261.
Irigaray, L. (1985) *This Sex Which is Not One*, trans. G. Gill, Ithaca, NY: Cornell University Press.
Jay, M. (1988) 'Scopic Regimes of Modernity', in H. Foster (ed.), *Vision and Visuality*, Seattle, WA: Bay Press, 3–23.
Jay, M. (1993) *Downcast Eyes. The Denigration of Vision in Twentieth-Century French Thought*, Berkeley, CA: University of California Press.
Junod, T. (2003) 'The Falling Man', *Esquire Magazine*. Available online at: http://www.esquire.com/features/ESQ0903-SEP_FALLINGMAN (accessed 5 July 2011).
Kahn, C. (2006) 'Plato on Recollection', in H. Benson (ed.), *A Companion to Plato*, Vol. 37, Malden, MA: Blackwell, 119–132.
Kant, I. (1789) *Critique of Pure Reason*, trans. W. Pluhar (1996), Indianapolis, IN: Hackett.
Kant, I. (1798) *Anthropology from a Pragmatic Point of View*, trans. M. Gregor (1974), Leiden: Kluwer.
Krauss, R. (1993) *The Optical Unconscious*, Cambridge, MA: MIT Press.
Kuiper, P.C. (1984) *Nieuwe neurosenleer*, Houten/Diegem: Bohn Stafleu Van Loghum.
Kunz, H. (1946) *Die Anthropologische Bedeutung der Phantasie*, Basel: Verlag für Recht und Gesellschaft.
Lacan, J. (1958–1959) *Le désir et son interpretation. Séminaire 1958–1959*, Internal document of the Association freudienne internationale.
Lacan, J. (1966) *Écrits*, ed. J.-A. Miller, Paris: Seuil.
Lacan, J. (1966–1967) *La logique du fantasme: Séminaire 1966–1967* (unauthorized transcript).
Lacan, J. (1968) *The Language of the Self. The Function of Language in Psychoanalysis*, trans. A. Wilden, Baltimore, MD: Johns Hopkins University Press.
Lacan, J. (1973) *Télévision*, Paris: Seuil.
Lacan, J. (1975) *Le Séminaire Livre XXII. RSI*, in *Ornicar?*, nos. 2–5.
Lacan, J. (1975–1976) *Le sinthome: Séminaire 1975–1976* (unauthorized transcript).
Lacan, J. (1988a) *The Seminar of Jacques Lacan, Book 1: Freud's Papers on Technique*, ed. J.-A. Miller, trans. J. Forrester, Cambridge: Cambridge University Press.
Lacan, J. (1988b) *The Seminar of Jacques Lacan, Book 2: The Ego in Freud's Theory and in the Technique of Psychoanalysis*, ed. J.-A. Miller, trans. S. Tomaselli, Cambridge: Cambridge University Press.
Lacan, J. (1991) *Le séminaire de Jacques Lacan, Livre 17: L'envers de la psychanalyse*, ed. J.-A. Miller, Paris: Seuil.
Lacan, J. (1992) *The Seminar of Jacques Lacan, Book 7: The Ethics of Psychoanalysis*, ed. J.-A. Miller, trans. D. Porter, London: Routledge.

Lacan, J. (1994) *Le séminaire de Jacques Lacan, Livre 4: La relation d'objet*, ed. J.-A. Miller, Paris: Seuil.

Lacan, J. (1996) 'On Freud's "Trieb" and the Psychoanalyst's Desire', in R. Feldstein, B. Fink and M. Jaanus (eds) *Reading Seminars 1 and 2. Lacan's Return to Freud*, Albany, NY: State University of New York Press, 417–419.

Lacan, J. (1998a) *Le séminaire de Jacques Lacan, Livre 5: Les formations de l'inconscient*, ed. J.-A. Miller, Paris: Seuil.

Lacan, J. (1998b) *The Seminar of Jacques Lacan, Book 11: The Four Fundamental Concepts of Psychoanalysis*, ed. J.-A. Miller, trans. A. Sheridan, New York: Norton & Co.

Lacan, J. (1999) *The Seminar of Jacques Lacan, Book 20: On Feminine Sexuality: The Limits of Love and Knowledge (Encore)*, ed. J.-A. Miller, trans. B. Fink, New York: Norton & Co.

Lacan, J. (2006) *Écrits. The First Complete Edition in English*, trans. B. Fink, New York: Norton & Co.

Lagache, D. (1964) 'Fantaisie, réalité, vérité', *Revue française de psychanalyse*, 28(4): 515–538.

Lakoff, G. (1995) 'Body, Brain, and Communication (interview by Iain A. Boal)', in J. Brook and I. Boal (eds), *Resisting the Virtual Life,* San Francisco, CA: City Lights Books, 115–129.

Lamm, L.J. (1993) *The Idea of the Past: History, Science and Practice in American Psychoanalysis*, New York: New York University Press.

Laplanche, J. and Pontalis, J.-B. (1986) 'Fantasy and the Origins of Sexuality', in V. Burgin, J. Donald and C. Kaplan (eds), *Formations of Fantasy*, London: Methuen, 5–34.

Laplanche, J. and Pontalis, J.-B. (1998) *Vocabulaire de la psychanalyse*, Paris: Presses Universitaires de France.

Laurent, É. (1995) 'Alienation and Separation (I) and (II)', in R. Feldstein, B. Fink and M. Jaanus (eds), *Reading Seminar 11. Lacan's Four Fundamental Concepts of Psychoanalysis*, Albany, NY: State University of New York Press, 19–38.

Leclaire, S. (1971) *Démasquer le réel. Un essai sur l'objet en psychalyse*, Paris: Seuil.

Llinás, R.R. (2001) *I of the Vortex*, Cambridge, MA: MIT Press.

Lyotard, J.-F. (1986) *The Postmodern Condition: Report on Knowledge*, trans. G. Bennington and B. Massumi, Manchester: Manchester University Press.

MacDougal, R. (2005) 'Identity, Electronic Ethos, and Blogs. A Technological Analysis of Symbolic Exchange on the New News Medium', *American Behavioral Scientist*, 49(4): 575–599.

Marini, M. (1992) *Jacques Lacan. The French Context*, New Brunswick, NJ: Rutgers University Press.

Metz, C. (1982) *The Imaginary Signifier. Psychoanalysis and the Cinema*, Bloomington, IN: Indiana University Press.

Miller, J.-A. (1996) 'Commentary on Lacan's Text "On Freud's 'Trieb' and the Psychoanalyst's Desire"', in R. Feldstein, B. Fink and M. Jaanus (eds), *Reading Seminars 1 and 2. Lacan's Return to Freud*, Albany, NY: State University of New York Press, 422–427.

Miller, J.-A. (1999a) 'Les six paradigmes de la jouissance', *La Cause Freudienne*, 42: 7–29.

Miller, J.-A. (1999b) 'L'acte entre intention et conséquence', *La Cause Freudienne*, 42: 7–16.

Miller, J.-A. (2000) 'Biologie Lacanienne et événement de corps', *La Cause Freudienne*, 44: 7–59.

Miller, J.-A. (2007) 'The Sinthome, a Mixture of Symptom and Fantasy', in V. Voruz and B. Wolf (eds), *The Later Lacan: An Introduction*, Albany, NY: State University of New York Press, 55–72.

Mirzoeff, N. (1999) *An Introduction to Visual Culture*, London: Routledge.

Modell, A.H. (1996) 'The Interface of Psychoanalysis and Neurobiology', Boston Colloquium for Philosophy of Science. Available online at: http://www.psychomedia.it/pm/science/psybyo/modell.htm (accessed 23 January 2011).

Modell, A.H. (2006) *Imagination and the Meaningful Brain*, Cambridge, MA: MIT Press.

Morris, H. (1993) 'Narrative Representation, Narrative Enactment, and the Psychoanalytic Construction of History', *International Journal of Psychoanalysis*, 74: 33–54.

Mulvey, L. (1989) *Visual and Other Pleasures*, Bloomington, IN: Indiana University Press.

Nasio, J.-D. (1987) *Les yeux de Laure. Transfert, objet a et topologie dans la théorie de Jacques Lacan*, Paris: Aubier.

Nasio, J.-D. (1998) *Five Lessons on the Psychoanalytic Theory of Jacques Lacan*, Albany, NY: State University of New York Press.

Nietzsche, F. (1979) 'On Truth and Lies in a Nonmoral Sense', trans. D. Breazale, in *Philosophy and Truth: Selections from Nietzsche's Notebooks of the Early 1870's*, New Jersey: Humanities Press.

Nobus, D. (2000) *Jacques Lacan and the Freudian Practice of Psychoanalysis*, London: Routledge.

Noel, J. (1997) 'Interpreting Aristotle's *Phantasia* and Claiming its Role within *Phronesis*'. Available online at: http://www.ed.uiuc.edu/EPS/PES-Yearbook/97_docs/noel.html (accessed 12 June 2009).

Nusselder, A. (2009) *Interface Fantasy. A Lacanian Cyborg Ontology*, Cambridge, MA: MIT Press.

Perron, R. (2001) 'The Unconscious and Primal Phantasies', *International Journal of Psychoanalysis*, 82: 583–595.

Perron, R. (2006a) 'Idea/Representation', in *International Dictionary of Psychoanalysis*. Available online at: http://www.enotes.com/psychoanalysis-encyclopedia/idea-representation (accessed 30 June 2011).

Perron, R. (2006b) 'Fantasy (Reverie)', in *International Dictionary of Psychoanalysis*. Available online at: http://www.enotes.com/psychoanalysis-encyclopedia/fantasy-reverie (accessed 4 July 2011).

Perron, R. (2006c) 'Phylogenesis', in *International Dictionary of Psychoanalysis*. Available online at: http://www.enotes.com/psychoanalysis-encyclopedia/phylogenesis (accessed 7 July 2011).

Perron-Borelli, M. (2001) *Les fantasmes*, Paris: Presses Universitaires de France.

Phillips, P. (2003) 'Spectatorship, Audience and Response', in J. Nelmes (ed.), *An Introduction to Film Studies*, London: Routledge, 91–128.

Pinker, S. (1994) *The Language Instinct: How the Mind Creates Language*, New York: HarperCollins.

Plato (1978) 'Symposium', in E. Hamilton and H. Cairns(eds.), *The Collected Dialogues of Plato*, Princeton, NJ: Princeton University Press, 526–574.

Quinet, A. (1995) 'The Gaze as an Object', in R. Feldstein, B. Fink and M. Jaanus (eds), *Reading Seminar 11. Lacan's Four Fundamental Concepts of Psychoanalysis*, Albany, NY: State University of New York Press.

Ragland, E. (1996) 'An Overview of the Real, with Examples from Seminar 1', in R. Feldstein, B. Fink and M. Jaanus (eds), *Reading Seminars 1 and 2. Lacan's Return to Freud*, Albany, NY: State University of New York Press, 192–211.

Ribettes, J.-M. (1984) 'La troisième dimension du fantasme', in C. Wiart (ed.), *Art et Fantasme*, Seyssel: L'or d'Atalante, 185–213.

Rilke, R.M. (1975) *Duinesian Elegies*, Chapel Hill, NC: University of North Carolina Press.

Rorty, R. (1979) *Philosophy and the Mirror of Nature,* Princeton, NJ: Princeton University Press.

Rose, J. (1986) *Sexuality in the Field of Vision*, London: Verso.

Roudinesco, E. (1990) *Jacques Lacan & Co. A History* of *Psychoanalysis in France, 1925–1985*, trans. J. Mehlman, London: Free Association Books.

Saussure, F. de (1916) *Course in General Linguistics*, ed. C. Bally and A. Sechehaye, trans. R. Harris (1983), London: Duckworth.

Schacter, D. and Scarry, E. (eds.) (1998) *Memory, Brain, and Belief*, Cambridge, MA: Harvard University Press.

Schokker, J. and Schokker, T. (2000) *Extimiteit*, Amsterdam: Boom.

Scruton, R. (1983) 'Fantasy, Imagination and the Screen', in *The Aesthetic Understanding. Essays in the Philosophy of Art and Culture*, London: Methuen, 127–135.

Simmons, J. (1995) 'Sade and Cyberspace', in J. Brook and I. Boal (eds) *Resisting the Virtual Life*, San Francisco, CA: City Lights, 145–159.

Singer, H. (2006) *9/11: The Falling Man* [documentary film].

Solano-Suárez, E. (2007) 'Identification with the Symptom at the End of Analysis', in V. Voruz and B. Wolf (eds), *The Later Lacan: An Introduction*, Albany, NY: State University of New York Press, 95–105.

Steiner, G. (1989) *Real Presences*, Chicago, IL: University of Chicago Press.

Suler, J. (1998) 'Mom, Dad, Computer: Transference Reactions to Computers', in *The Psychology of Cyberspace.* Available online at: http://www-usr.rider.edu/~suler/psycyber/comptransf.html (accessed 8 June 2010).

Surya, M. (1987) *Georges Bataille. La mort à l'oeuvre*, Paris: Garamont.

Thurston, L. (ed.) (2002) *Re-Inventing the Symptom. Essays on the Final Lacan*, New York: Other Press.

Turkle, S. (1984) *The Second Self. Computers and the Human Spirit*, New York: Simon & Schuster.

Turkle, S. (1995) *Life on the Screen. Identity in the Age of Internet*, New York: Simon & Schuster.

Van Haute, P. (2002) *Against Adaptation. Lacan's Subversion of the Subject*, New York: Other Press.

Van Haute, P. and Geyskens, T. (2004) *Confusion of Tongues: The Primacy of Sexuality in Freud, Ferenczi, and Laplanche*, New York: Other Press.

Verhaeghe, P. (1994) *Klinische psychodiagnostiek vanuit Lacans discourstheorie*, Leuven: Acco.

Verhaeghe, P. (1999) *Does the Woman Exist? From Freud's Hysteric to Lacan's Feminine*, London: Rebus Press.

Verhaeghe, P. (2001) 'Subject and Body. Lacan's Struggle with the Real', in *Beyond Gender. From Subject to Drive*, New York: Other Press, 65–97.

Verhaeghe, P. (2004) *On Being Normal and Other Disorders: A Manual for Clinical Psychodiagnostics*, New York: Other Press.

Verhaeghe, P. and Declercq, F. (2002) 'Lacan's Analytic Goal: *Le sinthome* or the Feminine Way', in L. Thurston (ed.), *Re-Inventing the Symptom. Essays on the Final Lacan*, New York: Other Press, 59–82.

Winnicott, D.W. (1971) *Playing and Reality*, London: Routledge.

Žižek, S. (1992) *Enjoy Your Symptom. Jacques Lacan in Hollywood and Out*, New York: Routledge.

Žižek, S. (1993) *Tarrying with the Negative. Kant, Hegel, and the Critique of Ideology*, Durham, NC: Duke University Press.

Žižek, S. (1997) 'Desire:Drive = Truth:Knowledge', *Umbr(a)*, 1: 147–152. Available online at: http://www.lacan.com/zizek-desire.htm. (accessed 23 June 2009).

Žižek, S. (1998) 'Kant and Sade: The Ideal Couple', *Lacanian Ink*, 13: 12–25.

Žižek, S. (1999a) 'Of Cells and Selves', in E. Wright and E. Wright (eds), *The Žižek Reader*, Oxford: Blackwell, 302–320.

Žižek, S. (1999b) *The Ticklish Subject. An Essay in Political Ontology*, New York: Verso.

Žižek, S. (2001) *On Belief*, London: Routledge.

Žižek, S. (2002) *Welcome to the Desert of the Real*, London: Verso.

Žižek, S. and Daly, G. (2003) *Conversations with Žižek*, Cambridge: Polity Press.

Zupančič, A. (1996) 'Philosopher's Blind Man's Buff', in R. Salecl and S. Žižek (eds), *Gaze and Voice as Love Objects*, Durham, NC: Duke University Press, 32–58.

Zupančič, A. (2000) *Ethics of the Real: Kant and Lacan*, London: Verso.

INDEX